SCHAUM'S *Easy* OUTLINES

PROGRAMMING
WITH C++

Other Books in Schaum's Easy Outline Series include:

SCHAUM'S *Easy* OUTLINES

PROGRAMMING WITH C++

BASED ON SCHAUM'S *Outline of Programming with C++* BY JOHN HUBBARD

ABRIDGEMENT EDITOR
ANTHONY Q. BAXTER

SCHAUM'S OUTLINE SERIES
McGRAW-HILL

New York San Francisco Washington, D.C. Auckland Bogotá
Caracas Lisbon London Madrid Mexico City Milan Montreal
New Delhi San Juan Singapore Sydney Tokyo Toronto

JOHN R. HUBBARD is Professor of Mathematics and Computer Science at the University of Richmond. He received his Ph.D. from The University of Michigan.

ANTHONY Q. BAXTER is Associate Professor of Computer Science and Director of Undergraduate Studies at the University of Kentucky, where he has taught since 1972. He received his B.S. and M.S. degrees from Union College in New York and his Ph.D. from the University of Virginia.

1 2 3 4 5 6 7 8 9 10 11 12 13 14 15 DOC DOC 9 0 9 8 7 6 5 4 3 2 1 0 9

ISBN 0-07-052713-X

Sponsoring Editor: Barbara Gilson
Production Supervisor: Tina Cameron
Editing Supervisor: Maureen B. Walker

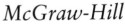

McGraw-Hill

A Division of The McGraw-Hill Companies

Contents

Chapter 1
INTRODUCTION TO C++ PROGRAMMING

IN THIS CHAPTER:

✔ *A Simple Program*
✔ *The Output Operator*
✔ *Characters, String Literals, and String Length*
✔ *Comments*
✔ *Variables, Objects, Declaration, and Initialization*
✔ *Simple Statements and the Assignment Operator*
✔ *Simple Arithmetic Operations*
✔ *Operator Precedence and Associativity*
✔ *The Increment and Decrement Operators*

✔ *Compound Assignment Statements*

✔ *Character, Integer, and Real Types*

✔ *Overflow, Underflow, and Roundoff Errors*

✔ *The E-Format for Floating-Point Values*

A program is a sequence of instructions for a computer to execute. Every program is written is some language. The C++ (pronounced see-plus-plus) is one of the most widely accepted programming languages available. It allows programmers to write efficient, well-structured, object-oriented programs.

This chapter introduces some of the basic C++ features.

A Simple Program

```
#include <iostream.h>
// This program displays "Hello World."
int main () {
    cout << "Hello World.\n";
    return 0;
}
```

The #include directive instructs the compiler to include the file iostream.h with our program. This file contains cout's definition. The second line is a comment and is ignored by the compiler. The third line contains the function prototype statement for the main function. This is required for every C++ program. The required parameter list is enclosed in parentheses ( ). In this example, we have no parameters. The opening and closing braces, { }, enclose the body of the main function.

The body of the main function is the `cout` statement: `cout <<` `"Hello World.\n";` which directs the computer to send the string `"Hello World.\n"` to the `cout` object. The `cout` object ("see-out") is the console output device that usually is the display screen. The `"\n"` in the string is the *newline* character. `"\n"` is a single character.

The `return 0;` causes `main` to return a zero value indicating to the operating system that it terminated normally.

The Output Operator

The symbol `"<<"` is called the *insertion operator*. It inserts objects into the output stream named on its left. The `cout` stream ordinarily refers to the monitor, so `cout <<123` would display the number `123`.

An *operator* is something that performs an action on one or more objects. The output operator `<<` performs the action of sending the value of the expression on its right to the object on its left. The expression values are directed out to the `cout` output *stream*. The reason that we call this a stream is that values sent to it fall in line, one after the other, as they are dropped into the stream.

The following all produce the same "Hello, World." output:
```
cout << "Hel" << "lo Wor" << "ld.\n";
cout << "He"  << "llo " << "World." <<"\n";
cout << "Hello" << " " <<"World" <<".\n";
```
Here the message has been split into several pieces. Since there are no newline characters or other characters added to the stream they all come out as a single line, just as before.

The output stream `cout` is used with the insertion operator `<<` in the general form:
```
cout <<expression <<expression ... <<expression;
```
This syntax statement says that `cout` is followed by one or more pairs, where each consists of the `<<` operator followed by some `expression`.

Characters, String Literals, and String Length

The symbol `'A'` is a character literal. It is a single character in length and is enclosed in a pair of single quotes. A *character* is any member of a predefined character set or alphabet. Most computers today use the ASCII (American Standard Code for Information Interchange) character set.

You Need to Know

Some additional non-printing characters such as the *newline* character, '\n', are also contained in the ASCII character set. The *backslash* character, '\', is used with a printing character to represent some useful non-printing characters. Some such characters are the *horizontal tab* character '\t', the *alert character* '\a', the quote character '\"', and the *backslash* character itself '\\'. Internally, a character requires one byte of storage.

The expression "Hello" is called a *string literal*. It consists of a sequence of characters delimited by quotation marks. The length of a string literal is the number of characters it contains. The string literal "ABCDE" has length 5. C++ provides a predefined function named strlen() that can be used to obtain the length of a string.

In the machine a C++ string of length n actually requires n + 1 bytes of memory for its storage. This is because the *null character* is appended after the last character in the string to indicate the end of the string. The null character is the character '\0'.

Note that the character 'a' requires one byte of storage and the string literal "a" requires two bytes; one for the 'a' and one for the terminating '\0'.

Example 1.1 Print String Lengths

```
#include <iostream.h>
#include <string.h>
// This program tests the strlen function
int main () {
    cout << strlen("Hello, World.\n") << '\n';
    cout << strlen("Hello, World.") << '\n';
    cout << strlen("Hello, ") << '\n';
    cout << strlen("H") << '\n';
    cout << strlen("") << '\n';
    return 0;
}
```

The `strlen()` function counts the characters in the specified string. The first two outputs would be 14 and 13 which demonstrates that the `'\n'` character counts as a single character. The last output demonstrates that the *empty string* has length 0.

Comments

Comments are messages in your program that are ignored by the compiler. They are messages intended for human readers of the program code.

There are two types of comments in C++. The *Standard C comment* begins with the combination slash-star symbol `/*` and ends with the star-slash symbol `*/`. Anything written between the opening `/*` and the closing `*/` is part of the comment. *Standard C comment*s can span several lines. The *Standard C++ comment* starts with a double slash `//` and continues to the end of the line. Most programmers prefer the C++ comment but the C comment is needed if you want to embed a C++ comment within a line of code.

Example 1.2 Demonstrate Comments

```
/********************************************\
 *    Sample Program with Comments          *
 *    Author:  A. Q. Baxter                  *
 *    Written: March, 1999                   *
\********************************************/
#include <iostream.h>
int main() {
  // here begins the program
  cout << "A message to output.\n";
  cout /* first */ << "Line 2\n";
  // This is the end of the program
  // The return statement is the best
  // way to end a C++ program
  return 0;  // all done
}
```

This program is clearly over commented but it contains all commenting styles. The initial five lines are a C comment as is the embedded comment in the second `cout` statement. The other comments are C++ comments. C++ comments extend only to the end of the line.

Variables, Objects, Declaration, and Initialization

A *variable* is a symbol that represents a storage location in the computer's memory. The information that is stored in that location is called the *value* of the variable. The most common way that a variable obtains a value is by means of an assignment. This has the syntax

> *variable = expression;*

The *expression* is first evaluated, and then its resulting value is assigned to the *variable*. The equal sign "=" is the *assignment operator*.

Example 1.3 Assignment and Variable Declaration

```
#include <iostream.h>
// assignment & declarations
int main() {
    int n, x;     // declare n and x
    n = 22;       // assign a value to n
    int y=33;     // declare y and assign a value
    x = 11;       // assign a value to x
    cout <<n <<" " <<x <<" " <<y <<endl;
    return 0;
}
```

The first line of the main program declares n and x to be of type int. The next line assigns a value of 22 to the variable n. The next line both declares the variable y to be of type int and assigns an initial value of 33 to y. The next line assigns a value of 11 to the variable x. Finally, we display the values of these three expressions n, x, and y. The endl in the cout statement is equivalent to the *endline* character '\n' and forces the output buffer to be "flushed" to the screen.

A declaration of a variable is a statement that gives information about a variable to the C++ compiler. Its syntax is:

> *type var1, var2, . . . , varN;*

The value stored inside the computer for these variables are sequences of bits (0's and 1's). The program interprets these bits as integers because the variables were declared to be ints.

where *type* is the name of some C++ type. For example, the declaration int x; tells the compiler two things: (1) the name of the variable is x, and (2) the variable has type int. Every variable must have a type. Its *type* tells the compiler how the variable is to be interpreted and what set of values can be assigned to it.

C++ is an *object-oriented* programming language Objects are endowed with certain capabilities. We say that the declaration *creates an object* and assigns a name to that object. Thus, int x; would create an object, name it x, and type it as int. We can visu-alize this by letting a shaded box represent that area in memory necessary to store that integer object to be used to represent the variable x. The question marks are to remind us that no value has yet been assigned to the variable. An assignment is one way that an object's value can be changed. In Ex. 1.3 the assignment x=11; changes the value of x to 11.

x

int

In C++ a declaration can be placed anywhere in a program, but it must be declared before it is used. As shown in Ex. 1.3, variables can be assigned an initial value when they are declared.

Simple Statements and the Assignment Operator

We have seen the use of the *assignment operator* (=). The assignment itself is an expression with a value. The value of the expression x = 22 is 22. Like any other value it can be used in another assignment: y = (x = 22); is an example of a *chained assignment*. First 22 is assigned to x and then the value of the assignment assignment 22 is assigned to y. Usually compound assignments are written without the parentheses.

Simple Arithmetic Operations

An *operator* is a symbol that "operates" on one or more expressions, producing a value. We have already encountered the output operator << and the assignment operator =.

Some of the simplest operators are those that do arithmetic. These operate on numeric types to produce another numeric type. For example, m + n produces the sum of m and n and -n produces the negation of n. Six operators are summarized in the following table.

Operator	Description	Example	Result for m = 38, n = 5
+	Add	m + n	43
−	Subtract	m − n	33
−	Negate	−m	−38
*	Multiply	m * n	190
/	Divide	m / n	7
%	Remainder	m % n	3

Note that 38/5=7 and 38%5=3. These two operations provide complete information about the ordinary division of 38 by 5: 38/5=7.6. The integer quotient 7 (38/5) and the integer remainder 3 (38%5) can be recombined with the dividend 38 and divisor 5 in the following relation: 7*5+3 = 38.

The integer quotient and remainder operators are more complicated if the integers are not positive. Of course, the divisor should never be zero. But if either is negative, m/n *always* gives the *same* result; m%n gives different results on different machines.

Operator Precedence and Associativity

Don't fight the system!
Know the precedence of Operations!

C++ has a rich repertoire of operators. (Appendix A lists all 55 of them.) Since an expression may include several operators, it is important to know in what order the evaluations of the operators occurs. We are already familiar with the precedence of ordinary arithmetic operators: the *, /, and % operators have higher precedence than the + and − operators; i.e., they are evaluated first. For example,

42-3*5 is evaluated as 42-(3*5) = 42-15 = 27

Moreover, all the arithmetic operators have higher precedence than the assignment and output operators. For example, the statement n=42- 3*5; will assign the value 27 to n. First the operator * is invoked to evaluate 3*5, then the - operator is invoked to evaluate 42-15, and then the operator = is invoked to assign 27 to n.

Part of Appendix B

Op	Description	Prec	Assoc	Arity	Example
–	Negate	15	Right	Unary	-n
*	Multiply	13	Left	Binary	m*n
/	Divide	13	Left	Binary	m/n
%	Remainder	13	Left	Binary	m%n
+	Add	12	Left	Binary	m+n
–	Subtract	12	Left	Binary	m-n
<<	Bit shift left, output	11	Left	Binary	cout <<n
=	Simple assignment	2	Right	Binary	m=n

It lists eight operators that apply to integer variables. They fall into five distinct precedence levels. For example, the negate operator - has precedence level 15, and the binary multiply operator * has precedence level 13, so negate is evaluated before multiply. Thus the expression m*-n is evaluated as m*(-n). Assignment operators have lower precedence than nearly all other operators, so they are usually performed last.

The column labeled "**Assoc**iativity" tells what happens when several <u>different</u> operators with the same precedence level appear in the same expression. For example, + and - both have precedence level 12 and are left associative, so the operators are evaluated from left to right. For example, in the expression 8-5+4 first 5 is subtracted from 8, and then 4 is added to that sum: (8-5)+4 = 3+4 = 7.

The column labeled "**Arity**" lists whether the operator is unary or binary. *Unary* means that the operator takes only one operand. For example, the negate operator - is unary. *Binary* means that the operator takes two operands. For example, the add operator + is binary.

The Increment and Decrement Operators

Of the many features C++ inherited from C, some of the most useful are the increment operator ++ and decrement operator −. These operators transform a variable into a statement expression that abbreviates a special form of assignment.

The pre-increment operator (++m) and the post-increment operator (m++) when used as a stand-alone expression statement are both equivalent to the assignment: m=m+1;. They simply increase the value of m by 1. Similarly, the expression statements −n and n− are both equivalent to the assignment: n=n-1;. They simply decrease the value of n by 1. (The increment operator ++ was used in the name "C++" because it "increments" the original C programming language; it has everything that C has, and more.)

When used as subexpressions (i.e., expressions within expressions), the pre-increment operation ++m is different from the post-increment operation m++. The pre-increment increases the variable first <u>before</u> using it in the larger expression, whereas the post-increment increases the value of the variable only <u>after</u> using the prior value of the variable within the larger expression.

Since the incrementing process is equivalent to a separate assignment, there are really two statements to be executed when the increment operation is used as a subexpression: the incrementing assignment and the larger enclosing statement.

 **Note!**

The difference between the pre-increment and the post-increment is simply the difference between executing the assignment before or after the enclosing statement.

Example 1.4 Pre-Increment and Post-Increment Operations

```
#include <iostream.h.
int main() {
    int m=66, n;
    n = ++m;
```

```
cout <<"m = " <<m <<", n = " <<n <<endl;
n = m++;
cout <<"m = " <<m <<", n = " <<n <<endl;
cout <<"m = " <<m++ <<endl;
cout <<"m = " <<m <<endl;
cout <<"m = " <<++m <<endl;
return 0;
}
```

```
m = 67, n = 67
m = 68, n = 67
m = 68
m = 69
m = 70
```

In the first assignment, m is pre-incremented, increasing its value to 67, which is then assigned to n. Next, m is post-incremented, so 67 is assigned to n and then m is increased to 68.

In the third output statement, m is post-incremented, so 68 is dropped into the output stream and then m is increased to 69. In the last output statement, m is pre-incremented to 70 and then that value is dropped into the output stream.

Compound Assignment Statements

C++ allows us to combine assignment with other types of operators. The general syntax for these combined assignments is: *variable op= expression,* where *op* is any binary operator. The effect of the combined assignment is: *variable = variable op expression.*

For example, the combined assignment number_so_far += 8; has the same effect as the simple statement:

```
number_so_far = number_so_far + 8;
```

Character, Integer, and Real Types

An integer is a whole number: 0, 1, -1, 2, etc. An unsigned integer is an integer that is not negative. C++ has the following integer types:

char	short int	unsigned short int
unsigned	int	unsigned int
unsigned char	long int	unsigned long int

The difference between these types is the range of values allowed. The ranges depend on the computer system being used. For example, on most PCs, `int` ranges between -32,768 and 32,767. On most UNIX workstations it ranges between -2,147,483,648 and 2,147,483,647. The `int` part may be omitted from `short int`, `unsigned short int`, `unsigned int`, `long int`, and `unsigned long int`.

C++ supports three real number types: `float`, `double`, and `long double`. Usually, `double` uses twice as many bytes as `float`. Typically, `float` uses 4 bytes, `double` 8 , and `long double` between 8 and 16 bytes.

Types that are used for real numbers are called "floating-point" types because of the way they are stored internally in the computer. On most systems, a number like 123.45 is first converted to binary form: `123.45=1111011.01110011`$_2$. Then the point is "floated" so that all the bits are on its right. In this example, the floating-point form is obtained by floating the point 7 bits to the left, producing a mantissa 2^7 times smaller. So the original number is

$$123.45 = 0.111101101110011 \cdot 2^7$$

This number would be represented internally by storing the mantissa `0.111101101110011` and the exponent 7 separately. For a 32-bit `float` type, the mantissa is stored in a 23-bit segment and the exponent in an 8-bit segment, leaving 1 bit for the sign of the number. For a 64-bit `double` type, the mantissa is stored in a 52-bit segment and the exponent in an 11-bit segment.

If you wished to determine how many bytes any particular machine uses for each type you can use the `sizeof` operator, which returns the size in bytes of the type specified. For example, `sizeof(unsigned short)` and `sizeof(double)` would evaluate to the number of bytes used to store an `unsigned short` and a `double`, respectively.

All floating-point arithmetic is done in `double` precision. So the only time you should use `float` instead of `double` is when you are storing large quantities of real numbers and are concerned about storage space or access time.

Overflow, Underflow, and Roundoff Errors

Unlike mathematical numbers, computer numbers are of finite precision. Integers have a finite range and floating-point numbers have limited precision and range. Attempts to increase a number above its maximum value will result in an *overflow* error. Decreasing a value below its smallest allowable value results in an *underflow*. Floating-point numbers are imprecise. This imprecision is called roundoff error.

Example 1.5 Roundoff Error

This program does some simple arithmetic to illustrate roundoff error:

```
void main() {
    double x=1000/3.0;      cout <<"x=" <<x;
    double y=x - 333.0;     cout <<"y=" <<y;
    double z=3*y - 1.0;     cout <<"z=" <<z;
}
```

```
x = 333.333   y = 0.333333   z = -5.68434E-14
```

In exact arithmetic, the variables would have the values $x=331/3$, $y=1/3$, and $z=0$. However, $1/3$ cannot be represented exactly as a floating-point value. The inaccuracy is reflected in the residue value for z.

This example also illustrates an inherent problem with using floating-point types within conditional tests of equality. If one were to test (z==0) it would <u>fail</u> even if z is very nearly zero, which is likely to happen when z should algebraically be zero. Therefore, it is better to avoid tests for equality with floating-point types.

The E-Format for Floating-Point Values

When input or output, floating-point values may be specified in either of two formats: *fixed-point* and *scientific*. The output in Ex. 1.5 illustrates both: 333.333 has fixed-point format, and -5.68434E-14 has scientific format.

Floating-point values with magnitude in the range 0.1 to 999,999 will normally be printed in fixed-point format; all others will be printed in scientific format.

Chapter 2
Conditionals and Type Conversion

In This Chapter:

- ✔ Input
- ✔ The if Statement
- ✔ The if...else Statement
- ✔ Relational Operators
- ✔ Compound Statements
- ✔ Keywords
- ✔ Compound Conditions
- ✔ Boolean Expressions
- ✔ Nested Conditionals
- ✔ The Conditional Expression Operator
- ✔ The switch Statement
- ✔ Scope

14

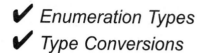

Enumeration Types
Type Conversions

The programs in Chapter 1 all have *sequential execution:* each statement in the program executes once, in the order that they are listed. Conditional statements allow for programs that are more flexible in that the execution of some statements depends upon conditions that change while the program is running.

This chapter describes the if statement, the if . . . else statement, and the switch statement and it also shows how to include simple input into your programs.

Input

In C++, input is analogous to output. Instead of data flowing out to the output stream cout, we have data flowing in from the input stream cin (pronounced "see-in"). The name stands for "console input."

Example 2.1 Integer Input
Here is code that reads integer input:

```
int main() {
    int age;
    cout <<"How old are you? ";
    cin  >>age;
    cout <<"In 10 yrs, you will be " <<age+10
            <<".\n";
    return 0;
}
```

```
How old are you? 19
In 10 yrs, you will be 29
```

The symbol >> is the *extraction operator,* also called the *input operator.* It is usually used with the cin input stream, which is usually the user's keyboard. Thus, when the statement cin >>age; executes, the system pauses, waiting for input. As soon as an integer is input, it is assigned to age and the program continues.

Note!

Notice that the preprocessor directive:

`#include <iostream.h>`

is missing from Ex. 2.1. It is required in any program that uses either `cin` or `cout`. Since nearly every program in this book uses either `cin` or `cout`, we will assume that you will include this line at the beginning of your source code file. Omitting it from these examples simply saves some print space. We will also omit the `return` statement at the end of the `main()` function in all future examples. We preface `main()` with `void` to indicate to the compiler that no `return` is expected.

The input object `cin` is analogous to the output object `cout`. Each is a C++ *stream* object that acts as a conduit through which bytes flow. The bytes flow into the running program through the `cin` object, and they flow out through the `cout` object.

Example 2.2 Character Input

```
void main() {
  char first, last;
  cout <<"Enter initials:\n";
  cout <<"\tFirst: ";
  cin >>first;
  cout <<"\tLast:   ";
  cin >>last;
  cout <<"Hi, " <<first <<". " <<last <<".!\n";
}
```

```
Enter initials:
     First: J
     Last: B
Hi, J. B.!
```

This example illustrates a standard way to format input. The first output line alerts the user to what general input is needed. This is followed by a sequence of specific input requests, called *user prompts*. Each user prompt is indented with the tab character `'\t'`, and by omitting the newline character `'\n'` it leaves the cursor on the same line for the user to enter a response there.

More than one variable may be read in the same input statement: `cin >>first >>last;` reads the items from left to right; *i.e.,* the leftmost variable is read first. Since the `char` type is an integer type, `cin` will ignore all leading *white space (i.e.,* blanks, tabs, and newlines) when it reads input. The input in this example could have been entered on several lines with leading and/or trailing blanks and tabs.

Notice that this prevents the input of blanks as characters using the input operator `<<`. In later chapters, we will see additional methods for character input.

The `if` Statement

The `if` statement allows conditional execution. Its syntax is

```
if (condition) statement;
```

where `condition` is an integer expression and `statement` is any executable statement. The `statement` will be executed only if the `condition` has a nonzero value. (Whenever an integer expression is being evaluated as a condition, a nonzero value is interpreted to mean "true" and a zero value to mean "false.") Notice the <u>required</u> parentheses around the `condition`.

Example 2.3 Testing for Divisibility

```
int n, d;
cout <<"Enter two integers: ";
cin >>n >>d;
if (n%d==0) cout <<d <<" divides " <<n <<endl;
```

```
Enter two integers: 24 6
6 divides 24
```

This code reads two integers and then checks the value of the remainder `n%d`. In this run, the value of `24%6` is 0, which means that 24 is divisible by 6. You will notice that we have omitted the void `main()` { and the closing }. Again this is to save space.

The trouble with this last example is that it doesn't do anything when n is not divisible by d so inputs of 6 and 24 produce no results.

To execute an alternative statement when the condition is zero, we need the `if ... else` statement.

The `if...else` Statement

The `if ... else` statement executes one of two alternative statements, according to the value of the condition. It has the syntax

```
if (condition) statement1;
else statement2;
```

where `condition` is an integer expression, and `statement1` and `statement2` are any statements. The `statement1` is executed if the `condition` has a nonzero value, and `statement2` is executed if the `condition` has a zero value.

Changing the `if` statement of Ex. 2.3 to:

```
if (n%d==0) cout <<d <<" divides " <<n <<endl;
else cout <<d <<" doesn't " <<n <<endl;
```

will produce output for all inputs.

A condition like `(n%d==0)` is an expression whose value is interpreted as being either "false" or "true." In C++ those two values are integers: 0 means "false," and any nonzero integer means "true." Because of that correspondence, conditions can be ordinary integer expressions. In particular, the integer expression `(n%d)` itself can be used as a condition. If it is nonzero (*i.e.,* "true") precisely when n is not divisible by d, we could reverse the two print statements in the previous example and rewrite it as:

```
if (n%d) cout <<d <<" doesn't divide " <<n <<endl;
else cout <<d <<" divides " <<n <<endl;
```

Relational Operators

Relational operators allow us to write conditions more intuitively. A condition, such as `(m>n)`, is an integer expression. If m is greater than n, the condition is "true" and evaluates to 1; otherwise, the condition is "false" and evaluates to 0.

The symbol `>` is one of the *relational operators*. It is called "relational" because it evaluates how the two expressions relate; for example, the relation 22>55 is false. The symbol is called an "operator" because when it is combined with expressions it produces a value. For example, when > is combined with 22 and 55 in the form 22>55, it produces the integer value 0, meaning "false."

You Need to Know

There are six relational operators:

<	less than	<=	less than or equal to
==	equal to	>	greater than
>=	greater than or equal to	!=	not equal to

Note the double equals sign == must be used to test for equality. A common error among C++ programmers is to use the single equals sign =. This mistake is difficult to uncover because it does not violate the syntax rules of C++.

Example 2.4 Finding the Maximum of Three Integers
This program prints the largest of the three numbers input:
```
int n1, n2, n3;
cout <<"Enter three integers: ";
cin >>n1 >>n2 >>n3;
int max=n1;
if (n2>max) max=n2;
if (n3>max) max=n3;
cout <<"The maximum is " <<max <<endl;
```

```
Enter three integers: 22 44 66
The maximum is 66
```

```
Enter three integers: 77 33 55
The maximum is 77
```

On the first run, n1 is 22, n2 is 44, and n3 is 66. First max is assigned 22. Then, since 44 > 22, max is assigned 44. Finally, since 66 > 44, max is assigned 66, and that value is printed. On the second run, n1 is 77, n2 is 33, and n3 is 55. First max is assigned 77. Then, since 33 is not greater than 77, max is unchanged. Finally, since 55 is also not greater than 77, max is again unchanged, and so the value 77 is printed.

Compound Statements

A *compound statement* is a sequence of statements that is treated as a single statement. C++ identifies a compound statement by enclosing its sequence of statements in curly braces. Here the braces enclose a three-statement *block*. As a compound statement, it is treated as a statement and can be used wherever any other statement could be used. (In a C++ program everything that follows main() is a compound statement.)

```
{ int temp = x;
    x = y;
    y = temp;
}
```

Example 2.5 Sorting

This program reads two integers and outputs them in increasing order:

```
int x, y;
cout <<"Enter two ints: ";
cin >>x >>y;
if (x>y) {
    int temp=x;
    x= ;
    y=temp;
}
cout <<x <<" " <<y <<endl;
```

```
Enter two ints: 66 44
44 66
```

The effect of putting this compound statement in the if statement is that all statements inside the block will be executed if the condition is true.

These three statements form a *swap*, interchanging the values of x and y. This construct is often used in programs that sort data.

The variable temp is declared inside the block. That makes it *local* to the block; *i.e.,* it only exists during the execution of the block. If the condition is false (x<y), then temp will never exist. This is an example of localizing objects so that they are created only when needed.

Example 2.5 is not the most efficient way to solve the problem. Its purpose is to illustrate compound statements and local variable declarations. If all we want to do is print the two numbers in increasing order; we could do it directly without the temp variable:

```
if (x<y) cout <<x <<" " <<y <<endl;
else cout <<y <<" " <<x <<endl;
```

Keywords

A *keyword* in a programming language is a word that is already defined and is reserved for a single special purpose. We have already seen the keywords char, else, if, int, long, short, signed, and unsigned. The remaining 40 keywords will be described subsequently. They are all described in Appendix A.

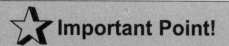 **Important Point!**

There are two kinds of keywords: those like if and else which serve as structure markers used to define the syntax of the language, and those like char and int which are actual names of things in the language. In some languages, the structure markers are called *reserved words* and the predefined names are called *standard identifiers.*

Compound Conditions

Conditions such as n%d and x>y can be combined to form compound conditions. The three *logical operators* that are used for this purpose are && (and), || (or), and ! (not). They are defined by

&&   p&&q is 1 only when both p and q evaluate to 1
|| p||q is 1 when either p or q or both evaluate to 1
!   !p is to 1 whenever p evaluates to 0

For example, (n%d || x>y) will be true if either n%d is nonzero or if x is greater than y (or both). !(x>y) is equivalent to x<=y and !(x<y) is equivalent to x>=y.

Definitions of the logical operators can be given by the *truth tables:*

p	q	p&&q
0	0	0
0	1	0
1	0	0
1	1	1

p	q	p||q
0	0	0
0	1	1
1	0	1
1	1	1

p	!p
0	1
1	0

These show, that if p has the value 1 (for "true") and q has the value 0 (for "false"), then the expression p&&q will have the value 0 and the expression p||q will have the value 1.

Example 2.6 The Maximum of Three Again

The same problem as Ex. 2.4 using compound conditionals:

```
int a, b, c;
cout <<"Enter three integers: ";
cin >>a >>b >>c;
if (a>=b && a>=c) cout <<a <<endl;
if (b>=a && b>=c) cout <<b <<endl;
if (c>=a && c>=b) cout <<c <<endl;
```

Note that Ex. 2.6 is no improvement over Ex. 2.4. Its purpose is simply to illustrate the use of compound conditionals.

Here is another example using a compound conditional:

Example 2.7 User-Friendly Input

This program allows the user to input either a Y or a y for "yes":

```
char ans;
cout <<"Are you enrolled (y/n): ";    cin >>ans;
if (ans=='Y'||ans=='y') cout <<"Enrolled.\n";
else cout <<"Not enrolled.\n";
```

```
Are you enrolled? N
Not enrolled.
```

It prompts the user for an answer, suggesting a response of either y or n. Then it accepts any character and concludes that the user meant "no" unless either a Y or a y is input.

Compound conditionals using && and || do not evaluate the second part of the conditional unless necessary. This is called *short-circuiting* or *lazy evaluation.* As the truth tables show, (p&&q) will be false if p is false. So there is no need to evaluate q if p is false. Similarly, if p is true, then there is no need to evaluate q to determine that (p||g) is true.

The value of short-circuiting is shown in the following example:

Example 2.8 Short-Circuiting in a Condition

This fragment tests integer divisibility:

```
int n, d;
cout <<"Enter two positive ints: ";
cin >>n >>d;
if (d>0&&n%d==0) cout <<d <<" divides " <<n <<endl;
else cout <<d <<" does not divide " <<n <<endl;
```

```
Enter two positive ints: 300 6
6 divides 300
```

```
Enter two positive ints: 300 7
7 does not divide 300
```

```
Enter two positive ints: 300 0
0 does not divide 300
```

In the first run, d is positive and n%d is zero, so the compound condition is true. In the second run, d is positive but n%d is not zero, so the compound condition is false. In the third run, d is zero, so the compound condition is determined to be false without evaluating the second component "n%d==0". This short-circuiting prevents the program from crashing because when d is zero the expression n%d cannot be evaluated.

Boolean Expressions

A *Boolean expression* is a condition that is either true or false. The expressions d>0, n%d==0, and (d>0 && n%d==0) are Boolean expressions. As we have seen, Boolean expressions evaluate to integer values where 0 means "false" and every nonzero value means "true."

Since all nonzero integer values are interpreted as meaning "true," Boolean expressions are often disguised. For example, the statement if (n%d) cout <<"n is not a multiple of d"; will print precisely when n%d is not zero. That happens when d does not divide n evenly, because n%d is the remainder from the integer division.

Boolean expressions having integer values can lead to some surprising anomalies in C++. For example, the following line might be written by a novice C++ programmer:

```
if (x >= y >= z) cout <<"max = x";    // ERROR!
```

Obviously, the programmer intended to write

```
if (x >= y && y >= z) cout <<"max  x";    // OK
```

The problem is that the erroneous line is syntactically correct, so the compiler will not catch the error. In fact, the program could run without any apparent error at all. This is a run-time error of the worst kind because there is no clear indication that anything is wrong.

The source of the difficulty described here is the fact that Boolean expressions have numeric values. Suppose that x and y both have the value 0 and that z has the value 1. The expression (x>=y>=z) is evaluated from left to right. The first part x>=y evaluates to "true" which is the numeric value 1. Then that is compared to z, and since they are equal the complete expression evaluates to "true" even though the author intended expression would be false!

The moral here is to remember that Boolean expressions have numeric values, and that compound conditionals can be tricky.

Another error that novice C++ programmers are prone to make is using a single equals sign when the double equals sign == should be used. For example,

```
if (x=0) cout <<"= 0";    // ERROR!
```
Obviously, the programmer intended to write
```
if (x==0) cout <<"x = 0";    // OK
```
The erroneous statement will first *assign* 0 to x. That assignment then has the *value* 0 which means "false" so the cout statement will not be executed. Even if x originally was zero, it will not be printed. Worse, if x originally was not zero, it will inadvertently be changed to zero!

Like the previous bug, this is another run-time error of the worst kind. It is very difficult to detect.

Nested Conditionals

Like compound statements, conditional statements can be used wherever any other statement can be used. So a conditional statement can be used within another conditional statement. This is called *nesting* conditional statements. For example, the condition in the last example could be restated equivalently as

```
if (d>0)
    if (n%d==0)   cout <<d <<" divides " <<n <<endl;
    else    cout <<d <<" doesn't divide " <<n <<endl;
    else
        cout <<d <<" doesn't divide " <<n <<endl;
```
Here extra indentation is used to help clarify the complex logic. Of

course, the compiler ignores all indentation and white space. To parse the statement, it uses the following "else matching" rule:

Match each `else` with the last unmatched `if`.

Using this rule, the compiler can easily decipher code as inscrutable as this:

```
        if (a>0) if (b>0) ++a; else if (c>0)
        if (a<4) ++b; else if (b<4) ++c; else —a;
        else if (a<4) —b; else —c; else a = 0;
```

To make it readable for humans, that code should be written like this:

```
if (a>0)
    if (b>0) ++a;
    else
        if (a>0)
            if (a<4) ++b;
            else
                if (b<4) ++c;
                else —a;
        else
            if (a<4) —b;
            else —c;
else
    a = 0;
```

Example 2.9 The Maximum of Three Again

Here is yet another way to do what was done in Exs. 2.4 and 2.6:

```
int a, b, c, max;
cout <<"Enter 3 int: ";
cin >>a >>b >>c;
if (a>b)
  if (a>c) max=a; // a>b and a>c
  else max=c;      // c>=a>b
else
  if (b>c) max=b; // b>=a and b>c
  else max = c;    // c>=b>=a
cout <<"The maximum is " <<max <<endl;
```

```
Enter 3 ints: 22 33 44
The maximum is 44

Enter 3 ints: 66 55 44
The maximum is 66
```

In the first run, the test (a>b) fails, so the second `else` executes the test (a>c), which also fails, thus executing the third else which assigns c to max. In the second run, both tests (a>b) and (a>c) succeed, so a is assigned to max. This program is more efficient than the one in Ex. 2.6 because it evaluates only two simple conditions instead of three compound conditions. Nevertheless, it should be considered inferior because its logic is more complicated.

> In the trade-off between efficiency and simplicity, one should opt for simplicity.

Nested conditionals by their very nature are complicated. It is usually better to avoid them if possible. An exception to this rule is a special form of nested conditional where all except possibly the last else is immediately followed by another if. This is a popular logical structure because it delineates in a simple way a sequence of disjoint alternatives. To clarify the logic, programmers usually line up the else if phrases, as shown in the next example.

Example 2.10

This program converts a number of years in college into a class name:

```
int yr;
cout <<"Enter class year: ";         cin >>yr;
if (yr<1) cout <<" *** not in school.";
else if (yr==1) cout <<" Freshman";
else if (yr==2) cout <<" Sophomore";
else if (yr==3) cout <<" Junior";
else if (yr==4) cout <<" Senior";
else cout <<" *** career student.";
```

```
Enter class year: 3 Junior
```

```
Enter class year: 1 Freshman
```

```
Enter class year: -9 *** not in school.
```

The year is tested through a cascade of conditionals, continuing until one is found true, or until the last else is reached as in the third run.

The Conditional Expression Operator

C++ provides an abbreviated form of a special case of the `if...else` statement. It is called the *conditional expression operator* and uses the `?` and the `:` symbols in a special ternary format:

```
condition ? expression1 : expression2
```

Like any operator, this combines the given expressions to produce a value. The value produced is either the value of `expression1` or that of `expression2`, according to whether the `condition` is true or false. For example, the assignment statement

```
min  = x<y ? x : y;
```

will assign the value of `x` to `min` if `x<y`, otherwise it assigns the value of `y` to `min`.

The conditional expression operator is generally used only when the condition and both expressions are very simple.

The `switch` Statement

The sequence of mutually exclusive alternatives delineated by the multiple `else if` construct often can also be coded using a `switch` statement. Its syntax is

```
switch (expression) {
    case constant1: statementList1;
    case constant2: statementList2;
        :
    case constantN: statementListN;
    default: statementList;
}
```

The `switch` statement evaluates the `expression` and then looks for its value among the case constants. If the value is found among the constants listed, then control is transferred to the first statement in that `statementList`. Otherwise if there is a default (which is optional), then the program branches to that `statementList`. Note that the `expression` must evaluate to an integer type and that the `constants` must be integer constants (which include `chars`).

Example 2.11

The program has the same effect as the program in Ex. 2.10:

```
int yr;
cout <<"Enter class year: ";      cin >>yr;
switch (yr<0 ? 0 : yr) {
   case 0: cout <<" *** not in school.";      break;
   case 1: cout <<" Freshman";                break;
   case 2: cout <<" Sophomore";               break;
   case 3: cout <<" Junior";                  break;
   case 4: cout <<" Senior";                  break;
   default: cout <<" *** career student.";
}
```

First the program changes negative years to 0 (yr<0 ? 0:yr) Then that value is located in the case list, and every statement from there to the next break is executed. If the breaks were not included every case after the matching one would be executed.

Scope

The *scope* of an identifier is that part of the program where it can be used. For example, variables cannot be used before they are declared, so their scopes begin where they are declared. Also a program may have several objects with the same name as long as their scopes are nested or disjoint. This is illustrated by the next example.

Example 2.12 Nested and Parallel Scopes

```
int x = 11;        // this x is global int main()
{                  // begin scope of main() int x =
22;
   {               // begin scope of internal block
      int x = 33, y=44;
      cout <<"In inside block: x = " <<x <<endl;
   }               // end scope of internal block
   cout <<"In main(): x = " <<x <<endl;
   cout <<"In main(): ::x = " <<::x <<endl;
   return 0;
}                  // end scope of main()
```

```
In inside block: x = 33
In main(): x = 22
In main(): :: x = 11
```

The variable y is only available in the inside block. There are three different objects named x in this program. The x that is initialized with the value 11 is a global variable, so its scope extends throughout the file. The x that is initialized to 22 has scope limited to main(). Since this is nested within the scope of the first x, it hides the first x within main(). The x that is initialized to 33 has scope limited to the internal block within main(), so it hides both the first and the second x within that block.

The last line in the program uses the *scope resolution operator* :: to access the global x that is otherwise hidden in main().

Enumeration Types

In addition to the predefined types such as int and char, C++ allows you to define your own data types. This can be done in several ways, the most powerful of which use classes as described in Chapters 8–11. We consider here a much simpler kind of user-defined type.

An *enumeration type* is a user-defined integral type with the syntax:

```
enum typename { enumeratorlist };
```

Here enum is a C++ keyword, typename stands for an identifier that names the type being defined, and enumeratorlist stands for a list of identifiers that define integer constants. For example, the following defines the enumeration type Semester, specifying three possible values that a variable of that type can have:

```
enum Semester {fall, spring, summer};
```

We can then declare variables of this type:

```
Semester s1, s2;
```

and can use them as we would predefined types:

```
s1 = spring; s2 = fall;
if (s1==s2) cout <<"Same semester.\n";
```

The actual values defined in the enumeratorlist are called *enumerators*. In fact, they are ordinary integer values. The values fall, spring, and summer defined for the Semester type above could have been defined like this:

```
const int fall=0, winter=1, summer=2;
```

The values 0, 1, . . . are assigned automatically when the type is defined. These default values can be overridden in the `enumeratorlist:`

```
enum Coin {penny=1,nickel=5,dime=10,quarter=25};
```

If integer values are assigned to only some of the enumerators, then the ones that follow are given consecutive values. For example,

```
enum Days {mon=1, tue, wed, thur, fri, sat, sun};
```

will assign the numbers 1 through 7 to the days of the week.

Enumeration types are usually defined to make code more *self-documenting; i.e.,* easier to understand. Here are a few more examples:

```
enum Boolean {false, true};
enum Gender {female, male};
enum Base {bin=2, octal=8, dec=10, hex=16};
enum Color {red, orange, yellow, green, blue};
enum Roman {I=1, V=5, X=10, L = 50, C=100, D=500};
```

Definitions like these can help make your code more readable. However, enumerations should not be overused. Each enumerator in an enumerator list defines a new identifier. For example, the definition of Roman above defines the seven identifiers I, V; X, L, C, D, and M as specific integer constants, so these letters could not be used for any other purpose within the scope of their definition.

Enumerators must be valid identifiers. The following is <u>invalid</u>:

```
enum Grade {F, D, C-, C, C+,. B-, B, B+, A-, A };
```

because the characters '+' and '-' cannot be used in identifiers.

Type Conversions

In many cases, C++ allows objects of one type to be used where another type is expected. This is called *type conversion.* The most common examples of type conversion are from one integer type to another and conversion from an integer type to a floating-point type.

The general idea is that one type may be used where another type is expected if the expected type has a higher "rank." For example, a char can be used where an int is expected because int has higher rank than char. An int can be used instead of a float for the same reason.

Example 2.13 Type Promotion

```
char c='A';
short m=22;
```

```
int n= c+m;
float x = c+m+n+2.222;
cout <<"n = " <<n <<endl;
cout <<"x = " <<x <<endl;
```

The char variable c is initialized with the integer value 65 (ASCII for the character 'A') and the short variable m is initialized with the integer value 22. In the assignment n=c+m, the operands c and m have different integral types. Their values are promoted to type int before the resulting value of 87 is assigned to n. The variable x receives the value 65 + 22 + 87 + 2.22 or 176.22.

Type promotion like this is quite common and usually occurs unnoticed. The general rule is that any integral type will be promoted to int whenever an integer conversion like this is necessary. An exception to that rule applies on compilers whose implementation of int does not cover all the values of the type being promoted. In this case, the integral type will be promoted to unsigned int instead.

Since enumeration types are integral types, integral promotion applies to them too. If x were a variable of some emumerated type, then the statement: cout <<"x = " <<x <<endl; would promote the value of x is promoted from the enumeration type to the type int before it is inserted into the output stream.

Promoting from integer to float is done as one would expect and is usually taken for granted. But converting from a floating-point type to an integral type is not automatic.

In general, if T is one type and v is a value of another type, then the expression T(v) converts v to type T. This is called *type casting*. For example, if expr is a floating-point expression and n is a variable of type int, then n = int(expr); converts the value of expr to type int and assigns it to n. The effect is to remove the real number's fractional part, leaving only its whole number part to be assigned to n. For example, 2.71828 would be converted to 2. Note that this is *truncating*, not *rounding*.

Example 2.14 Simple Type Casting
This program converts a double to an int:

```
double v=1234.56789;
int n=int(v);
cout <<"v=" <<v <<", n=" <<n <<endl;
```

The double value 1234.56789 is converted to the int value 1234.

Because it is so easy to convert between integer types and real types in C++, it is easy to forget the distinction between them. In general, integers are used for counting discrete things, while reals are used for measuring on a continuous scale. This means that integer values are exact, while real values are approximate.

In the C programming language, the syntax for casting v as type T is `(T)v`. C++ inherits this form also, so we could have done `n=int(v)` as `n=(int)v`.

Chapter 3
ITERATION

In This Chapter:

✔ *The* while *Statement*
✔ *The* do...while *Statement*
✔ *The* for *Statement*
✔ *The* break *Statement*
✔ *The* continue *Statement*
✔ *The* goto *Statement*
✔ *Constants, Variables, and Objects*

Iteration is the repetition of a statement or block of statements in a program. C++ has three iteration statements: the while statement, the do... while statement, and the for statement. Iteration statements are also called *loops* because of their cyclic nature.

The while Statement

The while statement has the syntax

```
while (condition) statement;
```

First the condition is evaluated. If it is nonzero (*i.e.*, true), the statement is executed and the condition is evaluated again. These two steps are repeated until the condition evaluates to zero (*i.e.*, is false). Note that parentheses are required around the condition.

Example 3.1 Printing Cubes

```
void main() {
   int n;
   cout <<"Enter >0 ints.\nTerminate with 0\n";
   cin >>n;
   while (n>0) {
      cout <<" cubed is " <<n*n*n <<"\n";
      cin >>n;
   }
}
```

```
Enter >0 ints.
Terminate with 0
2 cubed is 8
5 cubed is 125
0
```

First n is set to 2. The while statement tests the condition (n>0). Since the condition is true, the statements inside the loop are executed. The second statement reads 5 into n. At the end of the loop, control returns to the condition (n>0). It is still true, so the statements inside the loop are executed again. Each time control reaches the end of the loop, the condition is tested. After the third iteration, n is 0, and the condition is false. That terminates the loop.

Most C++ programmers indent all the statements that lie inside a loop to make it easier to see the logic of the program. When you want several statements to execute within a loop, you need to use braces { } to combine them into a compound statement. Example 3.1 illustrates the standard way to format a compound statement in a loop. The left brace ends the loop's header line. The right brace is on a line by itself below the "w" of the while keyword. And the statements within the compound statement are all indented.

Of course, the compiler doesn't care how the code is formatted. It would accept this format:

```
while(n>0){cout <<" cubed=" <<n*n*n <<"\n";cin >>n;}
```

Most C++ programmers find using multiple lines as in Ex. 3.1 to be easier to read. Some C programmers also like to put the left brace on a line by itself, directly below the "w" of the while keyword.

The do ... while Statement

The do ... while statement is almost the same as the while statement. Its syntax is

        do statement while (condition);

The only difference is that the do ... while statement executes the statement <u>first</u> and then evaluates the condition. These two steps are repeated until the condition evaluates to zero *(i.e.,* is false). A do ... while loop will always iterate at least once, regardless of the value of the condition, because the statement executes before the condition is evaluated the first time.

Example 3.2 The Factorial Function

This program computes the factorial function: $n!=(n)(n\text{-i}) \bullet \bullet \bullet (3)(2)\times(1)$.

```
void main() {
    int n, f=1;
    cout <<"Enter a positive integer: ";   cin >>n;
    cout <<n <<" factorial is ";
    do {
        f *= n;   n—;
    } while (n>1);
    cout <<f <<endl;
}
```

The program initializes f to 1 and then multiplies it by the input number n and all the positive integers that are less than n. So $5!=(5)(4)(3)(2)(l)=120$, and $8!=(8)(7)(6)(5)(4)(3)(2)(l)=40,320$.

The for Statement

A loop is controlled by three separate parts: an *initialization*, a *continuation condition*, and an *update*. For example, in the program in Ex. 3.2, the loop control variable is n; its initialization is cin >>n, its continuation condition is n>1, and its update is n—. When these three parts are simple, the loop can be set up as a for loop. The syntax for the for statement is

        for (initialize; continue; update)

The initialize, the continue, or the update may be empty.

If you have the choice between a `for` loop and a `while` or `do..`
`while` loop, you should probably use the `for` loop. As the next example illustrates, a `for` loop is usually easier to understand.

Example 3.3 The Factorial Function Again
Compare this program with the one in Ex. 3.2:

```
void main() {
    int n, f=1;
    cout <<"Enter a positive integer: ";  cin >>n;
    for (int i=2; i <= n; i++)  f *= i;
    cout <<n <<" factorial is " <<f <<endl;
}
```

This computes the factorial by multiplying 1 by the factors $2, 3, \ldots, n-i, n$. It won't run any faster than the version done with the `while` loop, but the code is more succinct.

It is customary to localize the declaration of the control variable in the initialization part of a `for` loop. For example, the control variable `i` in the program above is declared to be an `int` within the initialization part `int i=1`. This is a nice feature of C++. However, once the control variable is declared this way, it should not be redeclared in a later `for` loop. For example,

```
for (int i=0; i<100; i++) sum += i*i;
for (int i=0; i<100; i++) cout <<i; // ERROR
```

The same control variable can be used again; it just cannot be redeclared in the same block.

Example 3.4 The Extreme Values in a Sequence
This program reads a sequence of positive integers, terminated by a 0. It then prints the smallest and largest numbers in the sequence.

```
void main() {
    int n, min, max;
    cout <<"Enter >0 ints.\nTerminate with 0\n";
    cin >>n;
    for (min=max=n; n>0; ) {
        if (n<min) min=n;        //min-max are smallest
        else if (n>max) max=n; //& largest of the n
        cin >>n;                 // read so far
    }
    cout <<"min = " <<min <<"\nmax = " <<max <<endl;
}
```

```
Enter >0 ints.
Terminate with 0
55
22
88
66
0
min = 22
max = 88
```

Notice that the initialization part of the `for` loop `min=max=n` is the equivalent of two assignments, and the update part is empty.

A *sentinel* is a special value of an input variable that is used to terminate the input loop. In the example above, the value 0 is used as a sentinel.

Example 3.5 More than One Control Variable
This shows how a `for` loop may use more than one control variable:
```
void main() {
   for (int m=1, n=8; m<n; m++, n-)
      cout <<"m = " <<m <<", n = " <<n <<endl;
}
```
The initialization part of the `for` loop declares the two control variables m and n, initializing m to 1 and n to 8. The update part uses the comma operator to include two update expressions: m++ and n-. The loop continues as long as m<n.

The `break` Statement

We have already seen the `break` statement used in the `switch` statement. It is also used to terminate a loop.

Example 3.6 Breaking Out of an Infinite Loop
This `while` loop is equivalent to the one in Ex. 3.2:
```
while (1) {
    if (i>n) break;      // loop stops here when i>n
    sum += i*i;
    i++;
}
```
As long as (i<=n), the loop will continue. As soon as (i>n), the `break` statement executes, immediately terminating the loop.

Example 3.7 Controlling Input with a Sentinel
This program reads a sequence of positive integers, terminated by 0, and prints their average:

```
void main() {
  int n, count=0, sum=0;
  cout <<"Enter >0 ints.\nTerminate with 0\n";
  for ( ; ; ) {
    cout <<"\t" <<count + 1 <<": ";
    cin >>n;
    if (n==0) break;
    ++count;
    sum += n;
  }
  cout <<"Average is "
    <<float(sum)/count <<endl;
}
```

```
Enter >0 ints.
Terminate with 0
      1: 7
      2: 4
      3: 5
      4: 2
      5: 0
Average is 4.5
```

When 0 is input, the break executes and terminates the for loop causing the final output statement to execute. Without the use of the break here, the ++count statement would have to be put in a conditional or count would have to be decremented outside the loop or initialized to -1.

Notice that all three control parts of this for loop are empty: for(;;). This construct is pronounced "forever." Without the presence of the break, this would be an *infinite loop*.

The continue **Statement**

The break statement skips the rest of the statements in the loop and goes to the statement after the loop. The continue statement does the same thing except that, instead of terminating the loop, it goes back to the beginning of the loop to begin the next iteration.

Example 3.8 Using continue and break Statements
This program fragment illustrates the continue and break statements:

```
for (;;) {
    cout <<"Enter int: ";   cin >>n;
    if (n%2==0) continue;
    else if (n%3==0) break;
    cout <<" Loop Bottom.\n";
}
cout <<" Outside Loop.\n";
```

```
Enter int: 7
Loop Bottom
Enter int: 4
Enter int: 9
Outside loop
```

When n is 7, both of the `if` conditions fail and control reaches the bottom of the loop. When n is 4, the first `if` condition is true, so control skips over the rest of the statements in the loop and jumps to the top of the loop to continue with the next iteration. When n is 9, the first `if` condition is false but the second is true, so control breaks out of the loop and jumps to the first statement that follows the loop.

The `goto` Statement

The `break` statement, the `continue` statement, and the `switch` statement cause the control of the program to branch to a location other than where it normally would go. The destination of the branch is determined by the context: `break` goes to the next statement outside the loop, `continue` goes to the loop's continue condition, and `switch` goes to the correct case constant. All three of these statements are called *jump statements* because they cause the control of the program to "jump over" other statements.

The `goto` statement is another kind of jump statement. Its destination is specified by a label within the statement.

A *label* is simply an identifier followed by a colon, placed before a statement. Labels work like the `case` statements inside a `switch` statement: they specify the destination of the jump.

Example 3.9 Breaking Out of Nested Loops

This fragment illustrates the correct way to break out of nested loops.

```
for (int i=0; i<a; i++) {
    for (int j=0; j<b; j++)
        for (int k=0; k<c; k++)
```

```
        if (i*j*k>100) goto esc;
        else cout <<i*j*k <<" ";
esc: cout <<endl;
    }
```

When the `goto` is reached inside the innermost loop, program control jumps out to the output statement at the bottom of the outermost loop.

Another way to break out is to use a "done flag" within the continue conditions of the `for` loops like this:

```
int done=0;
for (int i=0; i<a && !done; i++) {
   for (int j=0; j<b && !done; j++)
      for (int k=0; k<c && !done; k++)
         if (i*j*k>100) done=1;
         else cout <<i*j*k <<" ";
}
```

This avoids the use of a `goto` but is a bit artificial and cumbersome.

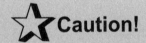

Caution!

The overuse of `goto` statements often produces unstructured spaghetti code that is difficult to debug, so limit your use of the `goto` statements to terminating deeply nested loops.

Constants, Variables, and Objects

An *object* is a contiguous region of memory that has an address, a size, a type, and a value. The *address* of an object is the memory address of its first byte. The *size* of an object is simply the number of bytes that it occupies. The *value* of an object is determined by the actual bits stored in its memory location and by the object's type that prescribes how those bits are to be interpreted.

The type of an object is determined by the programmer. The value of an object may be determined by the programmer at compile time or at run-time. An object's size is determined by the compiler and its address is determined by the computer's operating system at run-time.

Some objects do not have names. We will see examples of such anonymous objects later. A *variable* is an object that has a name. The word "variable" is used to suggest that the object's value can be changed. An object whose value cannot be changed is called a *constant*. Constants are declared by preceding the type specifier with the keyword const. Constants must be initialized when they are declared. The following program fragment illustrates constant definitions:

```
const char BEEP='\b';
const int MAXINT=2147483647;
int n=MAXINT/2;
const double PI=3.14159265358979323846;
```

Constants are usually defined for values that will be used more than once in a program but not changed.

> It is customary to use all capital letters in constant identifiers to distinguish them from other kinds of identifiers. A good compiler will replace each constant symbol with its numeric value.

Chapter 4
FUNCTIONS

IN THIS CHAPTER:

- ✔ *Standard C Library Functions*
- ✔ *User-Defined Functions*
- ✔ *Test Drivers*
- ✔ *Function Declarations and Definitions*
- ✔ *Separate Compilation*
- ✔ *Local Variables and Functions*
- ✔ `void` *Functions*
- ✔ *Boolean Functions*
- ✔ *I/O Functions*
- ✔ *Passing by Reference*
- ✔ *Passing by Constant Reference*
- ✔ *Scope*
- ✔ *Overloading*
- ✔ *The* `main()` *and* `exit()` *Functions*

✔ *Default Arguments*

To make large programs more manageable, we modularize them into subprograms called functions or methods. They can be developed, compiled, and tested separately and can be reused in other programs. This modularization is a characteristic of successful object-oriented software. Now we look at individual functions and in subsequent chapters we look at collecting groups of useful functions into classes.

Standard C Library Functions

The *Standard C Library* is a collection of predefined functions and other program elements that are accessed through *header files*. We have used some of these from the <iostream.h> header file. Our first example uses of one of the mathematical functions in <math.h>.

Example 4.1 The Square Root Function `sqrt()`
We can think of a function as a "black box" to which we send some values, called *arguments*, and which will use these arguments to compute and return a result. The sqrt function when given a positive number will return the value of the square root of the argument.

```
#include <iostream.h>
#include <math.h>
// Square root test driver.
void main() {
    for (int i=0; i<6; i++)
        cout <<i <<"\t" <<sqrt(i) <<endl;
}
```

This program prints the square root of the numbers 0,...,5. The #include <math.h> tells the compiler to use the functions defined in file math.h.

A function like sqrt() is executed by using its name as a variable in a statement, like this: y=sqrt(i)+10.0;

This is called *invoking* or *calling* the function. In the last example, sqrt(i) calls the sqrt function. The expression x in the parentheses is the *argument* or *actual parameter*. . So when i is 3, the value 3 is passed to the sqrt function by the call sqrt(i) . This process is illustrated by the following diagram:

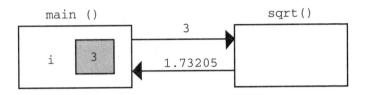

The variable i is declared in main(). During the fourth iteration of the for loop, its value is 3. That value is passed to the sqrt() function, which then returns the value 1.73205.

Example 4.2 Testing an Identity from Trigonometry

Here is code that uses <math.h> to allow an empirical verification of the standard trigonometric identity sin $2x=2$ sin $x$cos x:

```
#include <math.h>
//Fragment to test the identity sin2x=2sinx cosx:
for (float x=C; x < 2; x += 0.2)
    cout <<"\t" <<x; <<"\t\t" <<sin(2*x) <<"\t"
        <<2*sin(x)*cos(x) <<endl;
```

Executing this code would print x, sin 2 x, and 2 sin x cos x in three columns. Try it to see that for each value of x tested, sin2x=2sin$x$cos$x$. This provides empirical evidence of the truth of the identity.

Function values may be used like ordinary variables in an expression. Thus we can write

```
y=sqrt(2); or cout <<2*sin(x) *cos(x);
```

We can even "nest" function calls, like this:

```
y=sqrt(1 + 2*sqrt(3 + 4*sqrt(5)));
```

Most of the math functions you find on a pocket calculator are declared in the <math.h> header file, including those shown below.

Table 4.1 Some **<math.h>** Functions

Function	Description	Example
acos(x)	Inverse cosine (radians)	acos(0.2) returns 1.36944
asin(x)	Inverse sine of x (radians)	asin(0.2) returns 0.201358
atan(x)	Inverse tangent (radians)	atan(0.2) returns 0.197396
ceil(x)	Ceiling of x (rounds up)	ceil(3.141593) returns 4.0
cos(x)	Cosine of x (radians)	cos(2) returns -0.416147
exp(x)	Exponential of x (base e)	exp(2) returns 7.38906
fabs(x)	Absolute value of x	fabs(-2) returns 2.0

floor(x)	Floor of x (rounds down)	floor(3.141593) returns 3.0
log(x)	Natural log of x (base e)	log(2) returns 0.693147
log10(x)	Common log (base 10)	log10(2) returns 0.30103
pow(x,p)	x to the power p	pow(2,3) returns 8.0
sin(x)	Sine of x (radians)	sin(2) returns 0.909297
sqrt(x)	Square root of x	sqrt(2) returns 1.41421
tan(x)	Tangent of x (radians)	tan(2) returns -2.18504

Every mathematical function listed above returns a double type. If passed an integer, it is promoted to double before it is processed by the function.

Table 4.2 Some of the Header Files in the Standard C Library

Header File	Description
<assert.h>	The assert( ) function
<ctype.h>	Functions to test characters
<float.h>	Constants relevant to floats
<limits.h>	Integer limits on your local system
<math.h>	Mathematical functions
<stdio.h>	Functions for standard input and output
<stdlib.h>	Utility functions
<string.h>	Functions for processing strings
<time.h>	Time and date functions

These header files are used the same way as <iostream.h>. For example, if you want the random number function rand(), place #include <stdlib.h> at the beginning of your main program file.

User-Defined Functions

The functions provided by libraries are not sufficient for all problems. Programmers must be able to define their own functions.

Example 4.3 A cube() Function

Here is a simple example of a user-defined function:

```
// returns the cube of the given integer:
int cube(int x) {
```

```
      return x*x*x;
}
```

The `int` function returns the cube of the `int` argument, so `cube(2)` would return 8.

A user-defined function has two parts: its header and its body. The *header* of a function specifies its return type, name, and parameter list. In Ex. 4.3, the return type is `int`, the name is `cube`, and the parameter list is `int x`. Thus the header for the cube function is

```
      int cube(int x)
```

The *body* of a function is the block of code that follows its header. It contains the code that performs the function's action, including the return statement that specifies the value that the function sends back to the place where it was called. The body of the cube function is

```
      { return x*x*x; }
```

This body is about as simple as a function could have. Usually the body is much larger. But the function's header typically fits on a single line.

A function's *return statement* serves two purposes: it terminates the function, and it returns a value to the calling program. Its syntax is

```
      return expression;
```

where *expression* is any expression whose value could be assigned to a variable whose type is the same as the function's return type.

Test Drivers

Whenever you create your own function, you should test it with a simple program called a *test driver*. Its only purpose is to test the function. It is a temporary, *ad hoc* program that can be "quick and dirty." You need not include all the usual niceties of user prompts, output labels, and documentation.

Don't Forget!

Once you have used a test driver, discard it.

Example 4.4 A Test Driver for the `cube()` Function
Here is a program, with our cube function followed by a test driver:

```
// returns the cube of the given integer:
int cube(int x) { return x*x*x; }
// Test driver for the cube function:
main () {
    int n=1;
    while (n != 0) {
        cin >>n;
        cout <<cube(n) <<endl;
    }
}
```

This reads integers and prints their cubes until the user inputs the sentinel value 0. Each integer read is passed to the `cube` function by the call `cube(n)`. The value returned by the function replaces the expression `cube(n)` and is then passed to the output object `cout`.

Note that we omitted the `#include <iostream.h>` directive. This directive of course is required for every program that uses `cin` or `cout`. It is omitted from further examples only to save space.

We can visualize the relationship between the `main()` function and the `cube()` function like this:

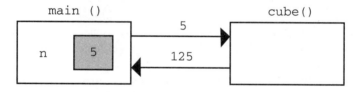

The `main()` function passes the value 5 to the `cube()` function, and the `cube()` function returns 125 to the `main()` function. The actual parameter n is passed by value to the formal parameter x. This simply means that x is assigned the value of n when the function is called.

Note that the `cube()` function is defined above the `main()` function in the example. This is because the C++ compiler must know about the `cube()` function before it is used in `main()`.

The next example shows a user-defined function named `max()`, which returns the larger of the two `int`s passed to it. This function has two arguments.

Example 4.5 A Test Driver for the `max()` Function

This function returns the larger of the two values passed to it:

```
int max(int x, int y) {
    return x<y ? y:x;
}
main() {
  int m,n;
    do
      cin >>m >>n;
      cout <<max(m,n) <<endl;
    } while (m!=0);
}
```

A `return` statement is like a `break` statement. It is a jump statement that jumps out of the function that contains it. Although usually found at the end of the function, a return statement may be put anywhere that any other statement could appear within a function.

Function Declarations and Definitions

The last two examples define a function in a program with the complete definition of the function listed above the main program.

Another, more common arrangement is to list only the function's header above the main program, and then list the function's complete definition (header and body) below the main program.

A function *declaration* or *prototype* is its header, followed by a semicolon. The *definition* is the complete function: header and body.

Like a variable declaration, a function declaration must appear above any use of its name. However, the function definition, when listed separately from the declaration, may appear anywhere outside the `main()` function and is usually listed after it or in a separate file.

You Need to Know

A function declaration is like a variable declaration. It provides the compiler with information needed to compile the rest of the file. The compiler doesn't need to know how the function works. It only needs the function's name, the number and types of its parameters, and its return type. This is the information contained in the function's header.

The variables that are listed in a parameter list are called *formal parameters* or *formal arguments*. They are local variables that exist only during the execution of the function. Their listing in the parameter list declares them. In Ex. 4.5, the formal parameters are x and y.

The variables that are listed in the function's calls are called the *actual parameters* or *actual arguments*. Like any other variable in the main program, they must be declared before they are used in the call. In Ex. 4.5, the actual parameters are m and n.

In these examples, the actual parameters are *passed by value*. This means that their values are assigned to the function's corresponding formal parameters. So in the previous example, the value of m is assigned to x and the value of n is assigned to y. When passed by value, actual parameters may be constants or expressions. For example, the max() function could be called by max(44, 5*m-n). This would assign the value 44 to x and the value of the expression 5*m-n to y.

Example 4.6 max() Function—Separate Declaration and Definition
This is the same test driver as Ex. 4.5. The function's declaration appears above the main program and its definition follows it:

```
int max(int, int);
//  test driver for the max function:
void main() {
    int m, n;
    do {
        cin   >>m >>n;
        cout <<max(m,n) <<endl;
    } while (m != 0);
}
// returns the larger of the two given integers:
int max(int x, int y) {
    if (x < y) return y; else return x;
}
```

Notice that the formal parameters, x and y, are listed in the header in the definition (as usual) but not in the declaration.

There is not much difference between a function declaration and a variable declaration, especially if the function has no parameters. For example, in a program that processes strings, you might need a variable named length to store the length of a string. However, a reasonable alternative would be to have a function that computes the length of the string wherever it is needed, instead of storing and updating the value. The function would be declared as `int length();` whereas the variable would be declared as `int length;`

The only difference is that the function declaration includes the parentheses ( ). In reality, the two alternatives are quite different, but syntactically they are nearly the same when they are used.

In cases like this one can regard a function as a kind of "active variable"; *i.e.*, a variable that can do things.

Separate Compilation

Function definitions are often compiled independently in separate files. For example, all the functions declared in the Standard C Library are compiled separately. One reason for separate compilation is "information hiding" — that is, information that is necessary for the complete compilation of the program but not essential to the programmer's understanding of the program is hidden. Experience shows that information hiding facilitates the understanding and thus success of large software projects.

Example 4.7 The `max()` Function Compiled Separately

```
// file test_max.cc
max(int, int);
// driver for max:
void main() {
  int m, n;
  do {
    cin >>m >>n;
    cout <<max(m,n) <<endl;
  } while (m != 0);
}
```

```
// file max.cc
// max=larger of two ints
int max(int x, int y) {
    return x<y ? y : x; }
```

`max()` (`max.cc`) and its test driver (`max_driver.cc`) are in separate files and could be compiled separately. The actual commands that you would use to compile these files will depend upon your local system.

Another advantage of compiling functions separately is that they can be tested separately before the program(s) that call them are written. Once you know that the `max` function works properly, you can forget about how it works and save it to be used whenever it is needed.

Yet another advantage of separate compilation is the ease with which one module can be replaced by another equivalent module. If you happen to discover a better way to implement max(), you can compile and test that function, and then link that module with whatever programs were using the previous version of the max() function.

Local Variables and Functions

A *local variable* is one declared inside a block. It is accessible only from within that block. Since the body of a function itself is a block, variables declared within a function are local to that function; they exist only while the function is executing. A function's formal parameters (arguments) are also regarded as being local to the function.

Example 4.8 The `factorial()` Function

```
int factorial(int n) {
   if (n < 0) return 0;
   int f = 1;
   while (n > 1) f *= n—;
   return f;
}
```

The factorial of a positive integer n ($n!$) is obtained by multiplying n by all the positive integers less than n: $n! = (n)(n - 1) \cdots \times(3)(2)(1)$.

This function has two local variables: n and f. The parameter n is local because it is declared in the function's parameter list. The variable f is local because it is declared within the function body.

 **Note!**

The use of local variables within functions is another example of information hiding. The user of a function need not know what variables are used within the function.

void Functions

A function need not return a value. In other programming languages, such a function is called a *procedure* or *subroutine*. In C++, such a function is identified by placing the keyword void as the function's return type. A void function is one that returns no value.

Since a void function does not return a value, it need not include a return statement. If it does have a return statement, then it appears simply as return; with no expression following the keyword return. In this case, the return statement is simply terminates the function.

A function with no return value is an action. Accordingly, it is usually best to use a verb phrase for its name.

Boolean Functions

Sometimes it is helpful to use a function to evaluate a condition, typically within an if or while statement. Such functions are called *Boolean functions*, after the British logician George Boole (1815–1864).

Example 4.9 A Function to Test Primality
This Boolean function tests whether a given integer is a prime number.

```
// returns 1 if p is prime, 0 otherwise
int isPrime(int p) {
   float sqrtp = sqrt(p);
   if (p<2) return 0;      // 2 is the first prime
   if (p==2) return 1;
   if (p%2 == 0) return 0; // 2 is the only even
prime
   for (int d=3; d<=sqrtp; d+=2)
       if (p%d == 0) return 0;
   return 1;
}
```

It works by looking for a divisor d of the given n. It tests divisibility with the condition (n%d==0). This is true when d is a divisor of n. In that case, n is not a prime number and the function returns 0. If the for loop finishes without finding any divisor it returns 1.

Once we get past the square root of n we stop because if n is a product d*a, one of the factors must be less than or equal to the square root of n. We define that to be a constant so that it is only evaluated once; if we had used `d<=sqrt(n)` to control the `for` loop, it would be reevaluated at the end of each iteration. It is also more efficient to check for even numbers (`n==2`) first. This way, the `for` loop need only check odd divisors by incrementing the divider `d` by 2 each iteration.

We have used name "`isPrime`" as its name to make its use more readable. `if (isPrime(n))` ... is almost the same as "if n is prime."

I/O Functions

Functions are particularly useful for encapsulating tasks that require messy details that are not very germane to the primary task of the program. For example, in processing personnel records, you might have a program that requires interactive input of a user's age. By relegating this task to a separate function, you encapsulate the details needed to ensure correct data entry without distracting the main program.

Ex. 4.10 illustrates an input function. The `while(1)` control of the loop in this example makes it look like an infinite loop: the condition (`1`) is always "true." But the loop is actually controlled by the return statement which terminates both the loop and the function.

Example 4.10 A Function for Reading the User's Age
This function that prompts the user for his/her age and then returns it. It is "robust" in the sense that it rejects unreasonable input. It repeatedly requests input until it receives an integer in the range 1 to 120:

```
int age() {
  int n;
  while(1) {
    cout <<"How old are you? ";  cin >> n;
    if (n<0) cout <<"\a\tAge can't be negative.";
    else if (n>120) cout <<"\a\tNot over 120.";
    else return n;
    cout << "\n\tTry again.\n";
  }
}
```

When acceptable input is received from `cin`, the function terminates with a return statement, sending the input back to the calling function. For unacceptable input (`n<0` or `n>120`), the system beep (`'\a'`) is sounded, and a comment is printed and the user is asked to "Try again."

This is an example of a function whose return statement is not at the end of the function.

Passing by Reference

So far, the parameters we have seen in functions have been *passed by value*. The expression used in the function call is evaluated first and the resulting value is assigned to the corresponding parameter in the parameter list before function execution. For example, in cube(x), if x is 4, then the value 4 is passed to the local variable n before the function executes. Since the value 4 is used locally inside the function, x is unaffected by the function. Thus, x is a *read-only* parameter.

The pass-by-value mechanism allows expressions to be passed to the function. For example, cube() could be called as cube(2*x-3) or even as cube(2*sqrt(x)-cube(3)). In each case, the expression is evaluated to a single value that is passed to the function.

Read-only, pass-by-value communication is usually what we want. It makes the function self-contained, protecting against accidental side effects. There are situations where a function must change the value of the parameter passed to it. This is done by passing it *by reference.*

To pass a parameter by reference, simply append an ampersand & to the type specifier in the parameter list. This makes the local variable a reference to the actual parameter passed to it. Therefore, the actual parameter is *read-write*, not read-only. Any change to the local variable inside the function will cause the same change to the actual parameter.

> Parameters passed by value are called *value parameters*, and those passed by reference are called *reference parameters*.

Example 4.11 The swap() Function
Swaps x and y so that each ends up with the other's value:

```
void swap(float& x, float& y) {
    float temp = x;
    x = y;
```

```
y  =  temp;
}
```

Its sole purpose is to interchange the two objects that are passed to it. This is accomplished by declaring the formal parameters x and y as reference variables: float& x, float& y. The reference operator & makes x and y synonyms for the actual parameters.

When a call swap(a,b) executes, the function creates its local references x and y so that x is an alias for a, and y is an alias for b. Then the local variable temp is declared and initialized with the value of a, a is assigned the value of b, and b is assigned the value of temp.

The compiler will accept float& x, float &x, float & x, or even float&x. It's a matter of taste.

Example 4.12 Passing by Value and Passing by Reference
This shows the difference between passing by value and by reference.
```
void f(int x, int& y) { x=88; y=99 }
main() {
    int a=22, b=33;
    cout <<"a = " <<a <<"  b = " << b << endl;
    f(a,b);
    cout <<"a = " <<a <<"  b = " << b << endl;
}
```
The call f(a,b) passes a by value to x and b by reference to y. So x is a local variable which is assigned a's value of 22, while y is an alias for the variable b whose value is 33. The function assigns 88 to x, but that has <u>no</u> effect on a. When it assigns 99 to y, it is really assigning 99 to b. Thus, when the function terminates, a still has its original value 22, while b has the new value 99. The actual parameter a is read-only, while the actual parameter b is read-write.

Table 4.3 Passing by Value versus Passing by Reference

Passing by Value	Passing by Reference
int x;	int &x;
Formal parameter *x* is local variable.	Formal parameter *x* is local reference.
A duplicate of the actual parameter.	A <u>synonym</u> for actual parameter.
Cannot change the actual parameter.	Can change the actual parameter.
Actual parameter may be constant, variable, or expression.	Actual parameter must be variable.
Actual parameter is read-only.	Actual parameter is read-write.

A common situation where reference parameters are needed is where the function has to return more than one value. It can only return one value directly with a return statement. So if more than one value must be returned, reference parameters can do the job.

Passing by Constant Reference

There are two good reasons for passing a parameter by reference. If the function has to change the value of the actual parameter, as the swap() function did, then it must be passed by reference. If the actual parameter takes up a lot of storage space (e.g., a one-megabyte graphics image), then it is more efficient to pass it by reference to prevent it from being duplicated. However, this also allows the function to change the value of the actual parameter. If you don't want the function to change its contents, C++ provides a third alternative: passing by *constant reference*. It works the same way as passing by reference, except that the function cannot change the parameter value. The effect is that the function has access to the actual parameter by means of its alias, but the value of parameter may not be changed during the execution of the function. A parameter that is passed by value is called "read-only" because it cannot change the contents of that parameter.

> Consider the function:
> ```
> void f(int x, int& y, const int& z)
> ```
> The first parameter is by value, the second parameter is by reference, and the third parameter is by constant reference.

Passing parameters by constant reference is used to process large objects, such as arrays and class instances that are described in later chapters. Objects of fundamental types (int, float, *etc.*) are usually passed by value (not modifiable) or by reference (modifiable).

Scope

The scope of a name consists of that part of the program where it can be used. It begins where the name is declared. If that declaration is inside a function (including main()), then the scope extends to the end of the innermost block that contains the declaration.

A program may have several objects with the same name as long as their scopes are nested or disjoint. This is illustrated below.

Example 4.13 Nested and Parallel Scopes

In this example, f() and g() are global functions, and the first x is a global variable with a scope of the entire file. This is called file *scope*. The second x is declared inside main() so it has *local scope; i.e.,* it is accessible only from within main(). The third x is declared inside an internal block, so its scope is restricted to that internal block.

```
void f();                          // f() is global
void g();                          // g() is global
int x = 11;                    // this x is global
main() {                   // begin scope of main()
  int x = 22;
  {                  // begin scope of internal block
    int x = 33;
    cout << "In block inside main(): " <<x <<endl;
  }                      // end scope of internal
block
  cout <<"In main(): x = " <<x <<endl;
  cout <<"In main(): ::x = " <<::x <<endl; //global x
  f();
  g();
}                          // end scope of main()
```

Each x scope overrides the scope of the previously declared x, so there is no ambiguity when the identifier x is referenced. The *scope resolution operator* :: is used to access the last x whose scope was overridden; in this case, the global x whose value is 11:

```
void f() {                      // begin scope of f()
  int x = 44;
  cout <<"In f(): x = " <<x <<endl;
}                          // end scope of f()
void g() {                      // begin scope of g()
```

```
cout <<"In g(): x = " <<x <<endl;
}                              // end scope of g()
```
The x initialized to 44 has scope limited to the f() which is parallel to main but its scope is also nested within the global scope of the first x, so its scope overrides that of both the first x within f(). The only place where the scope of the first x is not overridden is within the function g.

Overloading

C++ allows you to use the same name for different functions. As long as they have different parameter type lists, the compiler regards them as different functions. To be distinguished, the parameter lists must either contain a different number of parameters, or at least one position in their parameter lists must have different types.

Example 4.14 Overloading the max( ) Function
Here we define several max() functions in the same program:
```
int max(int, int);
int max(int, int, int);
double max(double, double);
void main()
   cout <<max(99,77) <<" " <<max(55,66,33) <<" "
        <<max(3.4,7.2) <<endl;
}
int max(int x, int y) {return (x > y ? x : y); }
int max(int x, int y, int z) {
   int t = (x>y ? x:y); return (z>t ? z:m); }
double max(double x, double y) {return (x>y ? x:y);
}
```
Three different functions, all named max, are defined here. The compiler checks their parameter lists to determine which one to use on each call. For example, the first call passes two ints, so the version that has two ints in its parameter list is called. (If that version had been omitted, then the system would promote the ints to doubles and pass them to the version that has two doubles in its parameter list.)

Overloaded functions are widely used in C++.

The `main()` and `exit()` Functions

Every C++ program requires a function named `main()`. In fact, we can think of the complete program itself as being made up of the `main()` function together with all the other functions that are called either directly or indirectly from it.

> Most C++ compilers expect the `main()` function to have return type `int`. Since this is the default return type for any function, it need not be specified. So we usually just write `main()` instead of `int main()`.

Some C++ programmers, as we have seen previously, prefer to declare `void main()` and any `return` statement should appear simply as `return,` since in this case `main()` has no return type.

If you want to terminate the program from within a function other than the main function, you cannot use a `return` statement. The `return` statement will only terminate the current function and return control to the invoking function. The `exit()` function that is defined in the `<stdlib.h>` header file takes an integer argument that is returned to the operating system as the "value" of the program execution. This value is usually ignored by the operating system unless the user is executing the program as part of a script.

Default Arguments

C++ allows a function to have a variable number of arguments. Providing default values for the optional arguments does this. Consider a function `p` with 4 double parameters. The first is required and the last three are optional:

```
double p(double, double=0, double=1, double=-1);
```
The call `p(1.2)` is equivalent to the call `p(1.2,0,1,-1)` and the call `p(x,7.6,5)` is equivalent to the call `p(x,7.6,5,-1)`.

In the example above, the function may be called with 1, 2, 3, or 4 arguments. So the effect of allowing default parameter values is really to allow a variable number of actual parameters passed to the function.

If a function has default parameter values, then the function's parameter list must show all the parameters with default values to the right of all the parameters that have no default values, like this:

```
void f(int a, int b, int c=4, int d=7, int e=3); //OK
void g(int a, int b=2, int c=4, int d, int e=3); //NO
```

The optional" parameters must all be listed last.

Chapter 5
ARRAYS

IN THIS CHAPTER:

✔ *Processing the Elements of an Array*

✔ *Initializing an Array*

✔ *Passing Arrays as Function Arguments*

✔ *C++ Does NOT Check the Range of an Array Index*

✔ *Multi-Dimensional Arrays*

✔ *Arrays with Enumeration Types*

✔ *Type Definitions*

An array is a sequence of objects all of the same type. The objects, called *elements*, are numbered consecutively starting with 0. These numbers are called *index values*, or *subscripts* of the array. Subscripts locate element positions and allow *direct access* into the array.

If the name of an array is a, then a[0] is the name of the first element — that element in position 0. Here is an array of 6 integers:

a	1	3	55	8	3	21
	a[0]	a[1]	a[2]	a[3]	a[4]	a[5]

Numbering the *i*th element with index $i - 1$ is called *zero-based indexing*. The index is the distance from the start of the array.

Processing the Elements of an Array

Processing arrays allows us to manipulate a list of objects without having to name each object differently. This example reads in a list of 4 data values and displays then in reverse order.

Example 5.1 Displaying a List of Values

```
main () {
  const int SIZE=4;
  double a[SIZE];
  cout <<"Enter " <<SIZE <<" reals:\n";
  for (int i=0; i<SIZE; i++) {
    cout <<i <<": ";
    cin >>a[i];
  }
  cout << "Here they are in reverse\n";
  for (i=SIZE-1; i>=0; i−) {
    cout <<"\ta[" <<i <<"]" = <<a[i] <<endl;
}
```

As is customary in C++ we have defined the array size as a separate constant. This allows changing a single line of code to alter the size of an array and all places where that size is used.

Initializing an Array

In C++ an array can be initialized with a single *initializer* list. We list the initial values for each element in the array and they are assigned to the array elements in the order they are listed. If the list is shorter than the array, the remaining array elements are filled with zeros (null characters for character types).

Example 5.2 Using an Array Initializer List

```
main () {
  const int SIZE=4;
```

```
    int a[SIZE] = {1,,5} ;
    for (int i = 0; i < SIZE; i++) {
        cout <<"a[" <<i <<"]"="" <<a[i] <<"   ";
}
```

```
a[0]=1   a[1]=0   a[2]=5   a[3]=0
```

Note that the uninitialized elements are set to zero. If we omitted the initializer list entirely, the results would be four "garbage" values of whatever happened to be in the memory used for the array.

Passing Arrays as Function Arguments

In C++ an array name is a symbolic reference to the memory location where the first element of the array is located. Some programming languages make the number of array elements available at execution time. The designers of C++ decided not to do this, so that the only attributes that are know about an array are the type of the elements and the location of the start of the array. The program in Ex. 5.3 illustrates how arrays are passed to functions.

Example 5.3 An Array I/O Function

```
const int SIZE = 100;
void getArr(double[], int&);
void dispArr(const double[], const int)
main () {
    double a[SIZE] = {1,,5} ;
    int n;
    getArray(a, n);
    cout <<"Array has " << n << " elements\n";
    dispArr(a, n);
}
void getArr (double x[], int& num) {
    num = 0;
    cout <<"Enter data (enter 0 to end):\n";
    do {
```

```
      cout << n << ": ";
      cin >> x[num++];
}
   while (x[num-1]!=0.0);
}
void dispArr(const double x[], const int num) {
   for (int i=0; i<num; i++)
      cout <<'\t' <<i <<": " <<x[i] <<endl;
}
```

The function getArr() changes the formal parameter num, so it is passed by reference. The formal parameter x is passed to the address of the first element of an array and that address is not changed, so it is declared as a const. Since x is the name of an array (indicated by x[]), the function can still change the array values.

C++ Does NOT Check the Range of an Array Index

Some languages will generate a run-time error if a program attempts to reference an array element with an index that is less than 0 or greater than the declared array size. The designers of C++ elected to leave this checking to the programmer.

If you attempt to access array elements with an index which is out of bounds, seemingly unpredictable results will occur. Since the array name references the location in memory where the array starts, a negative index will refer to memory located before the space reserved for the array. A positive index greater that the number of array elements will refer to memory above the array.

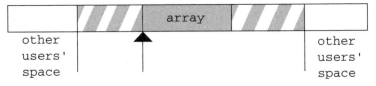

If the reference falls within the program's address space, the reference will be valid. If the reference reads data, it will probably reference a meaningless data item or program code. A write operation will overwrite some other data item or program instructions.

Note!

If the reference is outside the space owned by the executing program a *segmentation fault* (memory access violation) will occur and your program will terminate abnormally.

Multi-Dimensional Arrays

So far, we have looked only at *one-dimensional arrays*. Since the element type of an array may be any type, it can be an array type. An array of arrays is called a *multi-dimensional array*. A one-dimensional array of one-dimensional arrays is called a two-dimensional array; a one-dimensional array of two-dimensional arrays is called a three-dimensional array; etc. The simplest way to declare a multi-dimensional array is like this:

```
double a[32][10][4];
```

This is a three-dimensional array with dimensions 32, 10, and 4. The statement a[25][8][3] = 99.9 would assign the value of 99.9 to the element identified by the multi-index (25,8,3).

Example 5.4 An Array I/O Function

```
const int R=3, C=5;
void read(int [][C]);
void print (const int [][C]);
main () {
 int a[R][C];
 read(a);              print(a);
}
void read (int x[][C]) {
 cout <<"Enter " <<R*C <<"   " <<C <<"/row\n";
 for (int i=0; i<R; i++) {
  cout <<"Row " <<i << ": ";
  for (int j=0; j<C; j++) cin >> x[i][j];
 }
}
```

```
void print(const int x[][C]) {
  for (int i=0; i < R; i++) {
    cout "\nRow " <<i;
    for (int j=0; j<C j++) cout <<'\t' <<x[i][j];
  }
}
```

Notice that in the function's parameter lists, the first dimension is not specified while the second dimension (C) is specified. This is because the array a is stored as a one-dimensional array of R with each entry being an array containing C integers.

```
a[0][0], a[0][1], ..., a[0][C-1], a[1][0], a[1][1],
```
The computer doesn't need to know the number of rows, but it must know the length of each row (the number of columns) to be able to compute the distance from the first element to the one being accessed.

When a multi-dimensional array is passed to a function, the first dimension is not specified while all remaining dimensions are specified.

Example 5.5 Processing a Three-Dimensional Array
This counts the number of zeros in a three-dimensional array.
```
const int TBL=2, R=4, C=3;
int numZero(int X[][R][C], int n1,
                    int n2, int n3);
main() {
  int a[TBL][R][C]
    = { {{5,0,2},{0,0,9},{4,1,0},{7,7,7}},
        {{3,0,0},{8,5,0},{0,0,0},{2,0,9}} };
  cout <<numZero(a, TBL, R, C) <<" zeros.\n";
}
int numZero(int x[][R][C],
                    int t, int r, int c) {
  int count = 0;
  for (int i=0; i<t; i++)
    for (int j=0; j<r; j++)
      for (int k=0; k<c; k++)
        if (x[i][j][k]==0) count++;
  return count;
}
```

```
Array has 11 zeros.
```
Notice how the array is initialized: it is a two-element array of four-element arrays of three elements each.

Arrays with Enumeration Types

Enumeration types were discussed in Chapter 2. They are naturally processed with arrays. The following program fragment defines an array of seven real numbers, representing the high temperature for each of the seven days of a week:

Example 5.6 Days of the Week
```
enum Day{SUN, MON, TUE, WED, THU, FRI, SAT};
 double high[SAT+1] = {87.2, 81.0, 67.2,
             72.2, 75.5, 79.2, 81.5 };
 for (Day d=SUN; d<=SAT; d++)
   cout <<"\nDay " <<d <<" high=" <<high[d];
```

```
Day 0 high=87.2
Day 1 high=81.0
Day 2 high=67.2
Day 3 high=72.5
Day 4 high=75.5
Day 5 high=79.2
Day 6 high=81.5
```

A type Day variable can be assigned the values SUN, . . . , SAT and can be used the same way an int can. The array has dimension SAT+1 because we need seven elements and the value of SAT is 6. The loop takes the values of SUN, MON, . . . , SAT (0, 1, . . . 6). Using enumeration in this way makes your code more readable.

Type Definitions

As shown in the last section, enumeration is one way to define your own types. C++ also provides a way to rename existing types. The keyword typedef declares a new name (*i.e.*, an alias) for a specified type. A typedef does <u>not</u> define a new type; it only provides a synonym for an existing type. In Ex. 5.7 we use a typedef to name an array of doubles TempList.

Example 5.7 Days of the Week with typedef
```
#include <iostream.h>
typedef double TempList[];
enum Day{SUN, MON, TUE, WED, THU, FRI, SAT };
void disp(const TempList);
typedef TempDay Day;
```

```
main() {
   TempList high = {87.2, 81.0, 67.2, 72.2,
                               75.5, 79.2, 81.5};
   disp(high);
}
void disp (const TempList) {
 for (TempDay d=SUN; d<=SAT; d++)
   cout <<"\nDay " <<d <<" high was " <<high[d];
}
```

Observe that the array declaration TempList high shows us that the array specifier, [], is part of the definition. It is not needed in the declaration. The array has seven elements as the initializer specifies seven values. The variable d of type TempDay is actually of type Day. Finally, the formal parameter is specified as a TempList. This alerts us that the argument should be a list of temperatures, not just any array of doubles.

Chapter 6
POINTERS AND REFERENCES

When a variable is declared, three fundamental attributes are associated with it: its *name, type,* and *address* in memory. For example, the declaration int n; associates the name n, the type int, and the address of some location in memory where the value of n is to be stored. The value of a variable is accessed by means of its name. For example, we can print the value of n with the statement: cout <<n;

A variable's address is accessed by means of the *address operator* &. We can print the address of n with the statement: cout <<&n;

The address operator & "operates" on the variable's name to produce its address. It has precedence level 15 (*See* Appendix B) which is the same level as the logical NOT ! and pre-increment operator ++.

Example 6.1 Printing Pointer Values
This shows how the *value* and the *address* of a variable can be printed:
```
int n=33;
    cout <<" n=" <<n <<endl; //print value of n
    cout <<"&n=" <<&n <<endl;  //print address of n
```
You can tell that the second output 0x3fffd14 is an address by the "0x" prefix for hexadecimal format. This address is equal to the decimal number 67,108,116. Displaying a variable's address this way is not very useful. The address operator & has other more important uses. We saw one use in Chapter 4: designating reference parameters in a function declaration. That use is closely tied to another: declaring reference variables.

```
n=33
&n=0x3fffd14
```

References

A *reference* is an alias, a synonym for another variable. It is declared by appending the ampersand & to the reference's type.

Example 6.2 Using References
Here r is declared a reference for n:
```
    int n=33;
    int& r=n;        // r is a reference for n
    cout <<" n=" <<n <<",\t r=" <<r <<endl;      —n;
    cout <<" n=" <<n <<",\t r=" <<r <<endl;  r *= 2;
    cout <<" n=" <<n <<",\t r=" <<r <<endl;
    cout <<"&n=" <<&n <<",\t&r=" <<&r <<endl;
```

```
n=33,              r=33
 n=32,                    r=32
 n=64,             r=64
&n=0x3fffd14,  &r=0x3fffd14
```

The two identifiers n and r are different names for the same variable: they always have the same value. Decrementing n changes both n and r to 32. Doubling r increases both n and r to 64. The last line shows that r and n are *aliases*. The identifiers n and r are both symbolic names for the same memory location 0x3fffd14.

Like a const, a reference <u>must be initialized</u> when it is declared. That should seem reasonable: a synonym must have a something for which it is an alias. Every reference must have a referent.

Reference parameters were defined for functions in Chapter 4. We see that they work the same way as reference variables: they are synonyms for other variables.

Remember!

A reference parameter for a function is just a reference variable whose scope is limited to the function.

We have seen that the ampersand character & has several uses in C++. It can be used as a prefix to a variable name when it returns the address of that variable. When used as a suffix to a type in a variable declaration, it declares the variable to be a synonym for the variable to which it is initialized. When used as a suffix to a type in a function's parameter declaration, it declares the parameter to be a reference parameter for the variable that is passed to it. All of these uses are variations on the same theme: <u>the ampersand refers to the address</u> at which the value is stored.

Pointers

The reference operator & returns the address of the variable to which it is applied. We used this in Ex. 6.1 to print the address. We can also store the address in another variable. The type of the variable that stores an address is called a *pointer*. If the variable has type int, then the pointer variable must have type "pointer to int," denoted by int*:

The value of a pointer is an address that depends upon the state of the individual computer on which the program is running. In most cases, the actual value of that address is not relevant to the issues that concern the programmer. A pointer can be thought of as a "locator": it tells where to locate another value.

Often we will need to use the pointer p alone to obtain the value to which it points. This is called "dereferencing" the pointer, and is accomplished simply by applying the star * (the asterisk) symbol as an operator to the pointer. The address operator & and the dereference operator * are inverses of each other: n==*p whenever p==&n. This can also be expressed as n==*&n and p==&*p.

Example 6.3 Referencing and Dereferencing a Pointer

```
int n=33;
int* p=&n;    //   p points to n
cout <<"*p=" <<*p <<", ";
int& r=*p;    //   r is a reference for n
cout <<"r=" <<r <<endl;
```

Here p points to the integer named n, so *p and n are the same value;
`*p=33, r=33` *p is an alias for n. r is a reference to the value to which p points. So p references n and r dereferences p. Therefore, r is also an alias for n.

Derived Types

In Ex. 6.3, p has type pointer to int, and r has type reference to int. These types are derived from the int type. Like arrays, constants, and functions, these are *derived types*. Here are some declarations of derived types:

```
int& r=n;                   // r - reference to int
int* p=&n;                  // p - pointer to int
int a[]={33, 66};           // a - array of int
const int C=33;             // C - const int
int f()={ return 33; };     // f - function returns int
```

C++ types are classified as either fundamental or derived. The fundamental types include enumeration types and all the number types. Each derived type is based upon some other type. A variable declared to have any of the derived types illustrated above (constant, array, pointer, reference, and function) is based upon a single fundamental type.

You Need to Know

A derived type that is based upon more than one fundamental type is called a *structure type*. These include structures, unions, and classes.

Objects and lvalues

An *object* is a region of storage. An *lvalue* is an expression referring to an object or function. Originally, the terms "lvalue" and "rvalue" referred to things that appeared on the left and right sides of assignments. But now "lvalue" is more general. The simplest examples of lvalues are names of objects, *i.e.,* variables:

```
int n;
n=44;   // n is an lvalue
```

The simplest examples of things that are not lvalues are literals:

```
44=n;   // ERROR: 44 is not an lvalue
```

But, symbolic constants are lvalues:

```
const int MAX=65535; // MAX is an lvalue
```

even though they cannot appear on the left side of an assignment:

```
MAX=21024;   // ERROR: MAX is constant
```

Lvalues that can appear on the left side of an assignment are called *mutable lvalues;* those that can't are called *immutable lvalues.* Variables are mutable lvalues and constants are immutable lvalues. Other mutable lvalues include subscripted variables and dereferenced pointers:

```
int a[8];     a[5]=22;   // a[5] is a mutable lvalue
int* p=&n;    *p=77;     // *p is a mutable lvalue
```
Other immutable lvalues include arrays, functions, and references.

In general, an lvalue is anything whose address is accessible. Since an address is what a reference variable needs when it is declared, the C++ syntax requirement for such a declaration specifies an lvalue:

```
type& refname=lvalue;
```
For example, `int& r=n;` is legal, but right-hand sides of 44, n++, or `cube(n)` are all illegal lvalues.

Returning a Reference

A function's return type may be a reference if the value returned is an lvalue which is not local to the function. This restriction means that the returned value is actually a reference to an lvalue that exists after the function terminates. Consequently, that returned lvalue may be used like any other lvalue; for example, on the left side of an assignment:

Example 6.5 Returning a Reference

```
int& max(int& m, int& n) { //return ref. to int
  return (m > n ? m : n);   // m & n are nonlocal
}
void main() {
  int m=44, n=22;
  cout <<m <<", " <<n <<", " <<max(m,n) <<endl;
  max(m,n)=55;              // changes m from 44 to 55
  cout <<m <<", " <<n <<", " <<max(m,n) <<endl;
}
```

```
44, 22, 44
55, 22, 55
```

The `max()` function returns a reference to the larger of the two variables passed to it. Since the return value is a reference, the expression `max(m,n)` acts like a reference to `m` (since `m` is larger than `n`). So assigning 55 to the expression `max(m,n)` is equivalent to assigning it to `m` itself.

Arrays and Pointers

Although pointer types are not integer types, some integer arithmetic operators can be applied to pointers. The affect of this arithmetic is to cause the pointer to point to another memory location. The actual change in address depends upon the size of the fundamental type to which the pointer points.

Pointers can be incremented and decremented like integers. However, the increase or decrease in the pointer's value is equal to the size of the object to which it points.

Example 6.7 Traversing an Array with a Pointer

This example shows how a pointer can be used to traverse an array.

```
const int SIZE=3;
short a[SIZE]={22, 33, 44};
cout <<"a=" <<a <<endl;
cout <<"sizeof(short)=" <<sizeof(short) <<endl;
short* end=a + SIZE; // convert size to offset 6
short sum=0;
for (short* p=a; p < end; p++) {
   sum += *p;
   cout <<" p=" <<p;
   cout <<" *p=" <<*p;
   cout <<" sum=" <<sum <<endl;
}
cout <<"end=" <<end <<endl;
```

```
a=0x3fffd1a
sizeof(short)=2
 p=0x3fffd1a *p=22 sum=22
 p=0x3fffd1c *p=22 sum=22
 p=0x3fffd1e *p=22 sum=22
end=0x3fffd20
```

The second line of output shows that on this machine `short` integers occupy 2 bytes. Since `p` is a pointer to `short`, each time it is incremented it advances 2 bytes to the next `short` integer in the array. That way, sum+=*p accumulates the sum of the integers. If `p` were a pointer to `double` and `sizeof(double)` were 8 bytes, then each time `p` is incremented it would advance 8 bytes.

Example 6.7 shows that when a pointer is incremented, its value is increased by the number size (in bytes) of the object to which it points.

For example,
```
float a[8];
float* p=a;    // p points to a[0]        `
++p;           // increases p by sizeof(float)
```
If floats occupy 4 bytes, then ++p; increases the value of p by 4, and p+=5; increases the value of p by 20. This is how an array can be traversed: by initializing a pointer to the first element of the array and then repeatedly incrementing the pointer. Each increment moves the pointer to the next element of the array.

We can also use a pointer for direct access into the array. We can access a[5] by initializing the pointer to a[0] and then adding 5 to it:
```
float* p=a;    // p points to a[0]
p += 5;        // now p points to a[5]
```
So once the pointer is initialized to the starting address of the array, it works like an index.

WARNING: It is possible to access and modify unallocated memory locations.
```
float a[8];
float* p&a[7];   // p -> last a
++p;             // p -> past last!
*p=22.2;         // TROUBLE!
```

The next example shows an even tighter connection between arrays and pointers: the name of an array itself is a const pointer to the first element of the array. It also shows that pointers can be compared.

Example 6.8 Examining the Addresses of Array Elements
```
short a[]={22, 33, 44, 55, 66};
    cout <<"a=" <<a <<", *a=" <<*a <<endl;
    for (short* p=a; p<a+5; p++)
        cout <<"p=" <<p <<", *p=" <<*p <<endl;
```
Initially, a and p are the same: they are both pointers to short and they have the same value. Since a is a constant pointer, it cannot be incremented to traverse the array. Instead, we increment p and use the exit condition p<a+5. This computes a+5 to be that address 5 shorts past

`a[0];` which would by one short past the end of the array. The loop continues as long as p references an a not located past the last element.

The array subscript operator `[]` is equivalent to the dereference operator `*`. They provide direct access into the array the same way:

```
a[0] == *a
a[1] == *(a + 1)
a[2] == *(a + 2), etc.
```

So the array a could be traversed like this:

```
for (int i=0; i<5; i++)
    cout <*(a+i) <<endi;
```

Thus, pointers and array notation can be used interchangeably.

The new Operator

When the pointer is declared (e.g., float* p;) it only allocates memory for the pointer itself. The value of the pointer will be some memory address, but the memory referenced by that address is not yet allocated. This means that storage could already be in use by some other variable. In this case, p is uninitialized: it is not pointing to any allocated memory. Any attempt to access the memory to which it points will be an error:

```
*p=3.14159;    // ERROR: no storage for *p
```

A way to avoid this is to initialize pointers when they are declared:

```
float x=3.14159;   // x contains the value 3.14159
float* p=&x;       // p contains the address of x
cout <<*p          // OK: *p has been allocated
```

In this case, accessing `*p` is no problem because the memory needed to store the float 3.14159 was automatically allocated when x was declared; p points to the same allocated memory.

Another way to avoid the problem of a dangling pointer is to allocate memory explicitly. This is done with the new operator:

```
float* q;
q=new float; // allocate storage for 1 float
*q=3.14159;  // OK: *q has been allocated
```

The new operator returns the address of a block of s unallocated bytes in memory, where s is the size of a float. (Typically, `sizeof(float)` is 4 bytes.) Assigning that address to q guarantees that `*q` is not currently in use by any other variables.

The first two of these lines can be combined, thereby initializing q as it is declared: `float* q=new float;`

Note that using the `new` operator to initialize q only initializes the pointer itself, not the memory to which it points. It is possible to do both in the same statement that declares the pointer:

```
float* q=new float(3.14159);
cout <<*q;   // OK: both q and *q have been
                                    initialized
```

In the unlikely event that there is not enough free memory to allocate a block of the required size, the `new` operator will return 0 (the NULL pointer):

```
double* p=new double;
if (p == 0) abort();   // insufficient memory
else *p=3.141592658979324;
```

This prudent code calls an `abort()` function to prevent dereferencing the NULL pointer.

Consider again the two alternatives to allocating memory:

```
float x=3.14159;   // allocates named memory
float* p=new float(3.14159);   // allocates
                                    unnamed memory
```

In the first case, memory is allocated at compile time to the named variable x. In the second case, memory is allocated at run time to an unnamed object that is accessible through `*p`.

The delete Operator

The `delete` operator reverses the action of the `new` operator, returning allocated memory to the free store. It should only be applied to pointers that have been allocated explicitly by the `new` operator:

```
float* q=new float(3.14159);
delete q;        // deallocates q
*q=2.71828;   // ERROR: q has been deallocated
```

Deallocating q returns the block of `sizeof(float)` bytes to the free store, making it available for allocation to other objects. Once q has been deallocated, it should not be used again until after it has been reallocated.

Note!

A deallocated pointer, also called a *dangling pointer,* is like an uninitialized pointer: it doesn't point to anything.

A pointer to a constant cannot be deleted:

```
const int * p=new int;
delete p;   // ERROR: cannot delete pointer to
                                              const
```

This restriction is consistent with the general principle that constants cannot be changed.

Using the `delete` operator for fundamental types (`char`, `int`, `float`, `double`, *etc.)* is generally not recommended because little is gained at the risk of a potentially disastrous error:

```
float x=3.14159;   // x has value 3.14159
float* p=&x;   // p references x
delete p;   // RISKY: p not allocated by new
```

This would deallocate x, a mistake that can be very difficult to debug.

Dynamic Arrays

An array name is just a constant pointer allocated at compile time:

```
float a[20];   // a is a const pointer 20 floats
float* const p=new float[20];   // so is p
```

Here, both a and p are constant pointers to blocks of 20 floats. The declaration of a is called *static binding* because it is allocated at compile time; the symbol is bound to the allocated memory even if the array is never used while the program is running.

In contrast, we can use a non-constant pointer to postpone the allocation of memory until the program is running. This is generally called *run-time binding* or *dynamic binding*. An array that is declared this way is called a *dynamic array*. Compare the two ways of defining an array:

```
float a[20];                      // static array
float *p=new float [20];   // dynamic array
```

The static array a is created at compile time; its memory remains allocated thoughout the run of the program. The dynamic array p is created at run time; its memory allocated only when its declaration executes. Furthermore, the memory allocated to the array p is deallocated as soon as the delete operator is invoked on it:

```
delete [] p;   // deallocates the array p
```

The subscript operator [] must be included, because p is an array.

Example 6.9 Using Dynamic Arrays

The get() function here creates a dynamic array

```
void get(double*& a, int& n) {
   cout <<"Enter number of items: ";    cin >>n;
   a=new double[n];
   cout <<"Enter " <<n <<" items: ";
   for (int i=0; i<n; i++) cin >>a[i];
}
void print(double* a, int n) {
   for (int i=0; i < n; i++) cout <<a[i] <<" ";
   cout <<endl;
}
void main() {
   double* a;       // a is now an unallocated pointer
   int n;
// allocate it    use it         destroy it
   get(a, n);       print(a, n);  delete [] a;
   get(a, n);       print(a, n);  delete [] a;
}
```

```
Enter number of items: 4
Enter 4 items: 1.1 2.2
3.3 7.7
1.1 2.2 3.3 7.7
Enter number of items: 2
Enter 2 items: 1.23 9.87
1.23 9.87
```

Inside the get() function, n is obtained and the new operator allocates storage for n doubles. So the array is created "on the fly" while the program is running. Before get() is used to create another array for a, the current array has to be deallocated with the delete operator. Note that the subscript operator [] must be specified when deleting an array.

Note that the a is *a pointer that is passed by reference:*

```
void get(double*& a, int& n)
```

This is necessary because the new operator will change the value of a, which is the address of the first element of the newly allocated array.

Using const with Pointers

A pointer to a constant is different from a constant pointer. This distinction is illustrated in the following example.

Example 6.10 const Pointers, *etc*.
This fragment declares four variables: a pointer p, a constant pointer cp, a pointer pc to a constant, and a constant pointer cpc to a constant:

```
int n - 44;              // an int
int* p=&n;               // a pointer to an int
++(*p);                  // increments int *p
++p;                     // increment pointer p
int* const cp=&n;        // const pointer to int
++(*cp);                 // increments int *cp
++cp;                    // illegal:pointer cp is const
const int k=88;          // const int
const int * pc=&k        // pointer to a const int
++(*pc);                 // illegal:int *pc is const
++pc;                    // increments pointer pc
const int* const cpc=&k //const pntr to const int
++(*cpc);                //illegal:int *cpc is const
++cpc;                   //illegal:pointer cpc is const
```

Arrays of Pointers and Pointers to Arrays

The elements of an array may be pointers. Here is an array of 4 pointers to type double: double* p[4]; Its elements can be allocated like any other pointer: p[2]=new double(3.14159);

The next example illustrates a useful application of pointer arrays. It shows how to sort a list indirectly by changing the pointers to the elements instead of moving the elements themselves.

Example 6.11 Indirect Bubble Sort

```
void sort(float* p[], int n) {
  float* temp;
  for (int i=1; i < n; i++)
    for (int j=0; j < n-i; j++)
      if (*p[j] > *p[j+1]) {
        temp=p[j];
        p[j]=p[j+1];
        p[j+1]=temp;
      }
}
```

On each iteration of the inner loop, if the floats of adjacent pointers are out of order, then the pointers are swapped.

NUL, NULL, and void

The constant 0 (zero) has type int. Nevertheless, this symbol can be assigned to all the fundamental types. In each case, the object is initialized to the number 0. In the case of type char, the character c becomes the *null character;* denoted by '\0' or NUL.

The values of pointers are memory addresses. These addresses must remain within that part of memory allocated to the executing process, with the exception of the address 0x0. This is called the NULL pointer. The same constant applies to pointers derived from any type. All of the following initialize the pointers to NULL:

```
char* pc=0;        short* pd=0;   int* pn=0;
unsigned* pu=0;    float* px=0;   double* pz=0;
```

The NULL pointer cannot be dereferenced. This is a common <u>fatal error</u>:

```
int* p=0;

*p=22;  // ERROR: cannot dereference NULL pointer
```

A reasonable precaution is to test a pointer before attempting to dereference it:

```
if (p) *p=22; // ok
```

This tests the condition (p!=NULL) because that condition is true precisely when p is nonzero.

The name void denotes a special fundamental type. Unlike all the other fundamental types, void can only be used in a derived type:

```
void x;    // ERROR: no object can be void
void* p;  // OK
```

The most common use of the type void is to specify that a function does not return a value:

```
void swap(double&, double&);
```

Another, different use of void is to declare a pointer to an object of unknown type:

```
void* p=q;
```

This use is most common in low-level C programs designed to manipulate hardware resources.

Chapter 7
STRINGS

In This Chapter:

- ✔ *Review of Pointers*
- ✔ *Strings*
- ✔ *String I/O*
- ✔ *Some* `cin` *Member Functions*
- ✔ *Character Functions Defined in* `<ctype.h>`
- ✔ *Arrays of Strings*
- ✔ *The C-String Handling Library*

A *string* is a sequence of contiguous characters in memory terminated by the NUL character '\0'. Strings are accessed by variables of type char* (pointer to char). For example, if s has type char*, then cout << s << endl; will print all the characters stored in memory beginning at the address s and ending with the first occurrence of the NUL character.

The C header file <string.h> provides a wealth of special functions for manipulating strings. For example, the call strlen(s) will return the number of characters in the string s, not counting its terminating NUL character. These functions all declare their string parameters as pointers to char. So before we study these string operations, we need to review pointers.

Review of Pointers

A pointer is a memory address. The following declarations define x to be a float containing the value 44.44 and p to be a pointer containing the address of x:

```
float x = 44.44;
float* p = &x;
```

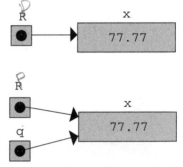

This shows two rectangles, one labeled p and one labeled x. The rectangles represent storage locations in memory. The variable p points to the variable x. We can access x through the pointer p by means of the dereference operator *. The statement

```
*p = 77.77;
```

changes the value of x to 77.77.

We can also have several pointers referencing the same object. Now *p, *q, and x are all names for the same object whose current value is 77.77.

If p is a pointer, then the call cout <<*p will <u>always</u> print the value of the object to which p points, and the call cout << p will <u>usually</u> print the value of the address that is stored in p. The important exception to this second rule is when p is declared to have type char*.

Strings

A C++ *string* is a character array with the following features:

- A NUL character `'\0'` is appended to the end of the array. This means that the number of characters in the array is always 1 more than the string length.
- The string may be initialized with a string literal like this:
  `char str[] = "Bethany";`
- Note that this array has 8 elements: `'B'`, `'e'`, `'t'`, `'h'`, `'a'`, `'n'`, `'y'`, `'\0'`.
- The entire string may be output as a single object, like this:
  `cout << str;` The system will copy characters from str to cout until the NUL character `'\0'` is encountered.
- The entire string may be input as a single object, like this:
  `cin >> buffer;` The system copies characters into buffer from cin until white space is encountered. The user must ensure that buffer is defined long enough to hold the input.
- The functions declared in `<string.h>` may be used to manipulate strings. These include the string length function `strlen()`, the string copying functions `strcpy()` and `strncpy()`, the string concatenating functions `strcat()` and `strncat()`, the string comparing functions `strcmp()` and `strncmp()`, and the token extracting function `strtok()`.

String I/O

Input and output of strings are done in several ways in C++ programs. The best way is by means of string class operators as described in Chapter 10. Since straightforward methods are useful to understanding how strings are represented and manipulated we describe these techniques in this chapter.

Example 7.1 Ordinary Input and Output of Strings
This fragment reads words into a 79-character buffer:
```
char word[80];
do
  cin >>word;  cout <<endl;
```

```
      if (*word) cout <<"\"" <<word <<"\"\n";
   } while (*word);
```

In this run, the `while` loop iterated 7 times: once for each word entered (including the **Ctrl-Z** that stopped the loop). Each word in the input stream `cin` is echoed to the output stream `cout`. The output stream is not "flushed" until the input stream encounters the end of line. Each string is printed with a double quotation mark on each side. This character must be designated by the character `'\"'`.

The expression `*word` controls the loop. It is the initial character in the string. It will be nonzero as long as the string `word` contains a string of length greater than 0. The string of length 0 (the empty or NUL string) contains a NUL (`'\0'`) as its first element. Pressing **Ctrl-Z** sends the end-of-file character in from `cin`. This loads the NUL string into `word`, setting `*word` (`word[0]`) to NUL and stopping the loop.

Note that punctuation marks (commas, periods, etc.) are included in the strings, but white space (blanks, tabs, newlines, etc.) is not.

The do loop in Ex. 7.1 could be replaced with:

```
cin >> word
while (*word) {
   cout <<"\"" <<word <<"\"\n";
   cin >> word;
}
```

When **Ctrl-Z** is pressed, the `cin` call assigns the empty string to `word`.

Example 7.1 illustrates that the output operator `<<` behaves differently with pointers of type `char*` than with other pointer types. With a `char*` pointer, `<<` outputs the character string to which the pointer points. With any other pointer type `<<` will output the pointer address.

Some `cin` Member Functions

The input stream object `cin` includes the input functions: `getline`, `get`, `ignore`, `putback`, and `peek`. Each of these functions is prefaced with the prefix "cin." when used because they are member functions of the object cin.

The call cin.getline(str,n) reads up to n characters into str and ignores the rest.

Example 7.2 The cin.getline() Function with Two Parameters
This fragment echoes the input, line by line:

```
char line[80];
do {
    cin.getline(line, 80);
    if (*line) cout << "[" << line << "]\n";
} while (*line);
```

```
The time has come, the walrus said,
[The time has come, the walrus said,]
to think of other things,
[to think of other things,]
^Z
```

(*line) becomes "true" when line contains a non-NUL string, because only then will line[0] be different from the NUL character.

The call getline(str,n,ch) reads input to the first occurrence of the delimiting character ch into str. If ch is the newline character '\n', then this is equivalent to getline(str, n). This is illustrated in the next example where the delimiting character is the comma.

Example 7.3 The cin.getline() Function
This program echoes the input, clause by clause:

```
char clause[30];
do {
    cin.getline(clause, 30, ',');
    if (*clause) cout << "  [" << clause << "]\n";
} while (*clause);
```

```
The time has come, the walrus said,
to think of other things,
^Z
  [The time has come]
  [the walrus said]
  [
to think of other things.]
[
```

The invisible end-line character that follows "said," is stored as the first character of the next input line. Since the comma is being used as the delimiting character, the endline character is processed just like an ordinary character.

get() is used for reading input character-by-character. The call get(ch) copies the next character from the input stream cin into the variable ch and returns 1, unless the end of file is detected in which case it returns 0. The opposite of get is put. put() is used for writing to the output stream cout character-by-character

The putback() function restores the last character read by a get() back to the input stream cin. The ignore() function reads past one or more characters in the input stream cin without processing them. Example 7.4 illustrates these functions.

Example 7.4 The `cin.putback()` and `cin.ignore()` Functions
This tests a function that extracts the integers from the input stream:

```
int nextInt();
void main() {
  int m=nextInt(), n=nextInt();
  cin.ignore(80,'\n');    //ignore rest of input line
  cout <<m <<" + " <<n <<" = " <<m+n <<endl;
}
int nextInt() {
  char ch;
  int n;
  while (cin.get(ch))
    if (ch>='0' && ch<='9') { //next char is a digit
      cin.putback(ch);    // replace so it can be
      cin >>n;            // read as a complete int
      break;
    }
  return n;
}
```

What is 305 plus 9416?
305 + 9416 = 9721

next_Int() scans past the characters until it encounters the first digit. In this run, that digit is 3. Since this digit will be part of the first integer 305, it is put back into cin so that the >> can read it into n.

peek() can be used in place of the combination get() and putback(). The call ch=cin.peek() copies the next character of the input stream cin into the char variable ch without removing that character from the input stream. The following code shows how peek() can be used in place of the get() and putback() functions.

```
while (ch = cin.peek())
    if (ch >= '0' && ch <= '9') {
        cin >> n;    break;
    }
    else cin.get(ch);
```

The expression ch=cin.peek() copies the next character into ch, and returns 1 if successful. Then if ch is a digit, the complete integer is read into n and returned. Otherwise, the character is removed from cin and the loop continues. If the end-of-file is encountered, the expression ch = cin.peek() returns 0, stopping the loop.

Character Functions Defined in <ctype.h>

Many character manipulation functions are defined in <ctype.h>; see Table 7.1.

Table 7.1 <ctype.h> Functions

isalnum()	int isalnum(int c); Returns nonzero if c is an alphabetic or numeric character; otherwise returns 0.
isalpha()	int isalpha(int c); Returns nonzero if c is an alphabetic character; otherwise returns 0.
iscntrl()	int iscntrl(int c); Returns nonzero if c is a control character; otherwise returns 0.
isdigit()	int isdigit(int c); Returns nonzero if c is a digit character; otherwise returns 0.
isgraph()	int isgraph(int c); Returns nonzero if c is any non-blank printing character; otherwise returns 0.
islower()	int islower(int c); Returns nonzero if c is a lowercase alphabetic character; otherwise returns 0.
isprint()	int isprint(int c); Returns nonzero if c is any printing character; otherwise returns 0.
ispunct()	int ispunct(int c); Returns nonzero if c is any printing character, except the alphabetic characters, the numeric characters, and the blank; otherwise returns 0.

isspace()	`int isspace(int c);` Returns nonzero if `c` is any white-space character, including the blank ` `, the form feed `'\f'`, the newline `'\n'`, the carriage return `'\r'`, the horizontal tab `'\t'`, and the vertical tab `'\v'`; otherwise returns 0.
isupper()	`int isupper(int c);` Returns nonzero if `c` is an uppercase alphabetic character; otherwise returns 0.
isxdigit()	`int isxdigit(int c);` Returns nonzero if `c` is a digit or one of hex letters: `'a',...,'f','A',...,'F'`; else returns 0.
tolower()	`int tolower(int c);` Returns lowercase of `c` if `c` is an uppercase alphabetic character; else returns `c`.
toupper()	`int toupper(int c);` Returns the uppercase version of `c` if `c` is a lowercase alphabetic character; otherwise returns `c`.

Note that these functions receive an `int` parameter `c` and they return an `int`. This works because `char` is an integer type. Normally, a `char` is passed to the function and the return value is assigned to a `char`, so we regard these as character-modifying functions.

Arrays of Strings

Recall that a two-dimensional array is really a one-dimensional array whose components themselves are one-dimensional arrays. When those component arrays are strings, we have an array of strings. The declaration `char name[5][40]` would allocate 200 bytes logically arranged in 5 rows of 40 characters each. We could use this to enter 5 names with the following code fragment:

```
for (int i=0; i<4; i++) cin.getline(name[i], 40);
```

The C-String Handling Library

The C header file `<string.h>` includes a family of functions that are very useful for manipulating strings. The simplest of these functions is the string length function `strlen()`. `strlen(s)` returns the integer length of the string referenced by s; that is, it counts the number of non-NUL from s until the first NUL character.

Strings are structured objects, composed of characters. So the operations that are provided for fundamental objects, such as the assignment operator (=), the comparison operators (<, >, ==, <=, >=, and !=), and the arithmetic operators (+, etc.) are not available for strings. Functions in the C-String Library simulate these operations.

The next example illustrates three other string functions. These are used to locate characters and substrings within a given string.

Example 7.5 The `strchr()`, `strrchr()`, and `strstr()` Functions

```
char s[] = "The Mississippi is a river.";
cout << "s=\"" << s << "\"\n";
char* p = strchr(s, ' ');
cout <<"strchr(s, ' ') -> s[" <<p-s <<"].\n";
p = strchr(s, 's');
cout <<"strchr(s, 's') -> s[" <<p-s <<"].\n";
p = strrchr(s, 's');
cout <<"strrchr(s, 's') -> s[" <<p-s <<"].\n";
p = strstr(s, "is");
cout <<"strstr(s, \"is\") -> s[" <<p-s <<"].\n";
p = strstr(s, "isi");
if (p == NULL)
    cout <<"strstr(s, \"isi\") is NULL\n";
```

```
s="The Mississippi is a river."
strchr(s, ' ') -> s[3].
strchr(s, 's') -> s[6].
strrchr(s, 's') -> s[17].
strstr(s, 'is') -> s[5].
strchr(s, 'isi') is NULL.
```

`strchr(s, ' ')` returns a pointer to the first occurrence of the blank character within s. The expression p-s computes the index 3 of this character within the string. (Remember the initial character `'T'` has index 0.) The character `'s'` first appears at index 6 in s.

The call `strrchr(s, 's')` returns a pointer to the <u>last</u> occurrence of the character `'s'`; this is at `s[17]`.

The call `strstr(s,"is")` returns a pointer to the first occurrence of the substring "is" within `s`; this is at `s[5]`. The call `strstr(s, "isi")` returns NULL because "isi" does not occur within `s`.

The functions that simulate string assignment are: `strcpy()` and `strncpy()`. `strcpy(s1,s2)` copies string `s2` into `s1`. `strncpy(s1, s2, n)` copies the first n characters of `s2` into `s1`. Both return `s1`.

Consider the following program fragment which illustrates the use of `strcpy()` and `strncpy()`:

```
char s1[] = "ABCDEFG";
char s2[] = "XYZ";
```

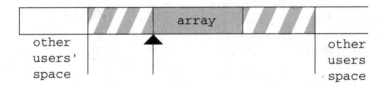

`strcpy(s1,s2);` replaces the characters starting at `s1` with characters starting at `s2` up to and including the terminating NULL character. Note that `strcpy(s1, s2)` creates a duplicate of string `s2`. The resulting two copies are distinct strings. Changing one of these strings later would have no effect upon the other string.

`strncpy(s1,s2,2);` applied to the original copy of `s1` replaces the first 2 characters of `s1` with XY, leaving the rest of `s1` unchanged. The effect of `strncpy(s1,s2,2)` can be visualized like this:

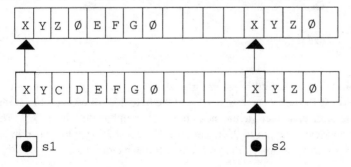

If n<strlen(s2) then strncpy(s1,s2,n) simply copies the first n characters of s2 into the beginning of s1. However, if n>strlen(s2), then strncpy(s1,s2,n) has the same effect as strcpy(s1,s2): it makes s1 a duplicate of s2 with the same length.

The strcat() and strncat() functions work the same as the strcpy() and strncpy() functions except that the characters from the second string are copied onto the end of the first string. The term "cat" comes from the word "catenate" meaning "string together."

The call strcat(s1, s2) to the original version of s1 appends XYZ onto the end of s1. It can be visualized like this:

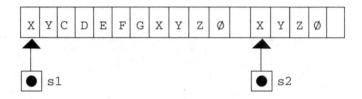

Since s2 has length 3, strcat(s1, s2) copies 4 bytes (including the NUL character), overwriting the NUL characters of s1 and its following 3 bytes. The length of s1 is increased to 10.

If any of the extra bytes following s1 that are needed to copy s2 are in use by any other object, the results will be unpredictable.

The call strncat(s1,s2,2) appends XY onto the end of s1. The effect can be visualized like this:

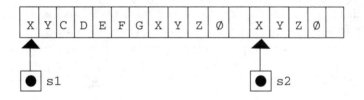

Since s2 has length 3, strncat(s1, s2, 2) copies 2 bytes, overwriting the NUL character of s1 and the byte that follows it. Then it puts the NUL character in the next byte to complete the string s1. This increases its length to 9. (If either of the extra 2 bytes had been in use by some other object, the program will behave unpredictably.)

The `strpbrk()` function uses a string of characters as a collection of characters. It generalizes the `strchr()` function, looking for the first occurrence in the first string of any of the characters in the second string.

Example 7.6 The `strpbrk()` Function

```
char s[]="The Mississippi is a river.";
cout <<"s = \"" <<s <<"\"\n";
char* p = strpbrk(s, "nopqr");
cout <<"strpbrk(s, \"nopqr\") -> s[" <<p-s <<"].\n";
p = strpbrk(s, "NOPQR");
if (p == NULL)
    cout <<"strpbrk(s, \"NOPQR\") is NULL\n";
```

The call `strpbrk(s, "nopqr")` returns the first occurrence in s of any of the five characters 'n', 'o', 'p', 'q', or 'r'. The first of these found is the 'p' at s[12].

The call `strpbrk(s, "NOPQR")` returns the NULL pointer because none of these five characters occurs in s.

Table 7.2 summarizes most of the useful functions in <string.h>. size_t is a special integer type that is defined in the <string.h> file.

Table 7.2 `<string.h>` Functions

memcpy()	void* memcpy(void* s1, const void* s2, size_t n); Replaces the first n bytes of *s1 with the first n bytes of *s2. Returns s1.
strcat()	char* strcat(char* s1, const char* s2); Appends s2 to s1. Returns s1.
strchr()	char* strchr(const char* s, int c); Returns pointer to the 1st occurrence of c in s. Returns NULL if c is not in s.
strcmp()	int strcmp(const char* s1, const char* s2); Compares s1 with substring s2. Returns a negative integer zero, or a positive integer, according to whether s1 is lexicographically less than, equal to, or greater than s2.
strcpy()	char* strcpy(char* s1, const char* s2); Replaces s1 with s2. Returns s1.
strcspn()	size_t strcspn(char* s1, const char* s2); Returns the length of the longest substring of s1 that begins with s1[0] and contains <u>none</u> of the characters found in s2.

`strlen()`	`size_t strlen(const char* s);` Returns the length of s, which is the number of characters beginning with `s[0]` that precede the first occurrence of the NUL character.
`strncat()`	`char* strncat(char* s1, const char* s2, size_t n);` Appends the first n characters of s2 to s1. Returns s1. If `n > strlen(s2)`, then `strncat(s1,s2,n)` is the same as `strcat(s1,s2)`.
`strncmp()`	`int strncmp(const char* s1, const char* s2, size_t n);` Compares first n characters of s1 with first n characters of s2. Returns a negative, zero, or a positive integer, according to whether the first substring is <, ==, or > the second. If `n > strlen(s2)`, then it is the same as `strcmp(s1,s2)`.
`strncpy()`	`char* strncpy(char* s1, const char* s2, size_t n);` Replaces the first n characters of s1 with the first n characters of s2. Returns s1. If `n < strlen(s1)`, the length of s1 is not affected. If `n > strlen(s2)`, then it is same as `strcpy(s1,s2)`.
`strpbrk()`	`char* strpbrk(const char* s1, const char* s2);` Returns the address of the first occurrence in s1 of any of the characters in s2. Returns NULL if none of the characters in s2 appears in s2.
`strrch()`	`char* strrchr(const char* s, int c);` Returns a pointer to the last occurrence of c in s. Returns NULL if c is not in s.
`strspn()`	`size_t strspn(char* s1, const char* s2);` Returns the length of the longest substring of s1 that begins with `s1[0]` and contains only characters found in s2.
`strstr()`	`char* strstr(const char* s1, const char* s2);` Returns the address of the first occurrence of s2 as a substring of s1. Returns NULL if ch is not in s1.
`strtok()`	`char* strtok(char* s1, const char* s2);` Tokenizes the string s1 into tokens delimited by the characters found in string s2. After the initial call `strtok(s1, s2)`, each successive call `strtok(NULL, s2)` returns a pointer to the next token found in s1. These calls change the string s1, replacing each delimiter with the NUL character `'\0'`.

Chapter 8
CLASSES

A *class* is is a derived type whose elements are other types. Unlike an array, the elements of a class may have different types. Furthermore, elements of a class may be functions, including operators.

Although any region of storage may generally be regarded as an "object," the word is usually used to describe variables whose type is a class. Thus, "object-oriented programming" involves programs that use classes. We think of an object as a self-contained entity that stores its own data and owns its own functions. The functionality of an object gives it life in the sense that it "knows" how to do things on its own.

There is more to object-oriented programming than just including classes in your programs, but that is the first step. An adequate treatment of the subject is far beyond this introductory outline.

Class Declarations

Here is a declaration for a class to represent rational numbers:

```
class Rational {
public:
    void assign(int, int);
    double convert();
    void invert();
    void print();
private:
    int num, den;
};
```

The declaration begins with the keyword `class` followed by the name of the class and ends the semicolon. This class is named `Rational`.

The functions `assign()`, `convert()`, `invert()`, and `print()` are called *services* or *methods*. The variables `num` and `den` are called *member data.*

In this class, all the methods are designated as `public`, and all the member data are designated as `private`. `Public` members are accessible from outside the class, while `private` members are accessible only from within the class. Preventing outside access is called "information hiding." It allows the programmer to modularize software, making it easier to understand, to debug, and to maintain.

Example 8.1. shows how `Rationals` are implemented and used.

Example 8.1 Implementing the Rational Class

```
class Rational {
public:
    void assign(int, int);
    double convert();
    void invert();
```

```
   void print();
private:
   int num, den;
};
void main() {
   Rational x;
   x.assign(22,7);
   cout <<"x = ";   x.print();
   cout <<" = " <<x.convert() <<endl;
   x.invert();
   cout <<"1/x = ";   x.print();   cout <<endl;
}
void Rational::assign(int n, int d)
       {num = n; den = d;}
double Rational::convert()
       {return double(num)/den;}
void Rational::invert()
       {int temp = num;   num = den; den=temp;}
void Rational::print()
       {cout <<num <<'/' <<den;}
```

Here x is declared as an object of the Rational class. Consequently, it has its own internal data members num and den, and it has the ability to call the class methods assign(), convert(), invert(), and print(). Note that a method like invert() is called by prefixing its name with the name of its owner: x.invert(). Indeed, a method can only be called this way. We say that the object x "owns" the call.

An object like x is declared as a variable but with type Rational. We think of this as a "user-defined type." C++ allows us to extend the programming language definition by adding our Rational type to the predefined types like int, float, *etc*. We visualize the object x below:

Notice the use of the specifier Rational: as a prefix to each method. This is necessary for each method definition that is given outside of its definition. The *scope resolution operator* is used to tie the function definition to the Rational class. Without this specifier, the compiler would not know that the function being defined is a method of the Rational class. This

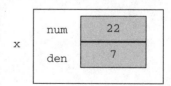

can be avoided by including the function definitions within declaration, as shown in Ex. 8.2.

When an object like the `Rational` object x in Ex. 8.1 is declared, we say that the class has been *instantiated,* and we call the object an *instance* of the class. And just as we may have many variables of the same type, we may have may instances of the same class:

```
Rational x, y, z;
```

Example 8.2 A Self-contained Implementation of `Rational`
The `Rational` class with its method definitions within the declaration:

```
class Rational {
public:
    void assign(int n, int d)
        {num=n; den=d;}
    double convert()
        {return double(num)/den;}
    void invert()
        {int temp=num; num=den; den=temp;}
    void print()
        {cout <<num <<'/' <<den;}
private:
    int num, den;
};
```

In most cases, the preferred style is to define the methods outside the class declaration, using the scope resolution operator as shown in Ex. 8.1. This physically separates the declarations from their definitions, consistent with the principle of information hiding. In fact, the definitions are usually put in a separate file and compiled separately. The point is that application programs need only know <u>what</u> the objects can do; they do not need to know <u>how</u> the objects do it. The function declarations tell what they do; the function definitions tell how they do it. This is how the predefined types (`int`, `double`, *etc.)* work.

Remember!

When the definitions are separated from the declarations, the declaration section is called the *class interface,* and the definition section is called the *implementation.* The interface is the part of the class that the programmer needs to see in order to use the class.

Constructors and Initialization Lists

The `Rational` class defined in Ex. 8.1 uses the `assign()` function to initialize its objects. It is more natural to allow initialization when the objects are declared. That's how ordinary (predefined) types work:

```
int n = 22;
char* s = "Hello";
```

C++ uses constructor functions to allows this style of initialization. A *constructor* is a method that is invoked automatically when an object is declared. A constructor function has the same name as the class itself and it is declared without a return type. Ex 8.3 illustrates how we can replace the `assign()` function with a constructor.

Example 8.3 A Constructor Function for the `Rational` Class

```
class Rational {
public:
   Rational(int n, int d)          {num=n; den=d;}
   void print()            {cout <<num <<'/' <<den;}
private:
   int num, den;
};
```

We can now declare rationals as `Rational x(-1,3), y(22,7);` the function of which has the same effect as the `assign()` function had in Ex. 8.1. When the declaration of x executes, the constructor is called automatically and the integers -1 and 3 are passed to its parameters n and d and assigned to x's `num` and `den` data members. A class's constructor "constructs" the class objects by allocating and initializing storage for the objects.

A class may have many constructors. Like all overloaded functions, they are distinguished by having distinct parameter lists. For example:

```
Rational()                          {num=0;  den=1;}
Rational(int n)                     {num=n;  den=1;}
Rational(int n,  int d)             {num=n;  den=d;}
```

The first has no parameters and initializes the declared object with the default values 0 and 1. The second has one int parameter and initializes the object to be the fractional equivalent of that integer. The third constructor is the same as in Ex. 8.3.

Among the various constructors that a class may have, the simplest is the one, called the *default constructor*, has no parameters. If this constructor is not explicitly declared in the class definition, the system will automatically create one. That is what happens in Ex. 8.1.

These could also be written equivalently using *initialization lists* as:

```
Rational(): num(0), den(1) { }
Rational(int n): num(n), den(1) { }
Rational(int n, int d): num(n), den(d) { }
```

Note that the list begins with a colon and precedes the function body. These three separate constructors are not necessary. They could be combined into a single constructor, using default parameter values:

```
Rational(int n=0, int d=1): num(), den(d) { }
```

In the declaration: Rational x, y(4), z(22,7); x will represent 0/1, y will represent 4/1, and z will represent 22/7.

Recall that the default values are used when actual parameters are not passed. In the declaration of the Rational object x, the formal parameters n and d are given default values of 0 and 1, respectively. In the declaration of the object y, n is given that value 4 and d is given the default value 1. No default values are used in the declaration of z.

Access Functions

Although a class's member data are usually declared private to limit access, it is also common to include public methods that provide read-only access to the data. Such functions are called *access functions*.

Example 8.4 Access Functions in the Rational Class

```
class Rational {
public:
   Rational(int n=0, int d=1) : num(n), den(d)   { }
   int numerator() const                {return num;}
   int denominator() const              {return den;}
private:
   int num, den;
};
void main() {
   Rational x(22,7);
   cout <<x.numerator() <<'/'
        <<x.denominator() <<endl;
}
```

The functions numerator() and denominator() return the values of the private member data. The const keyword in the declarations of the two access functions allows them to be applied to constant objects.

Private Methods

Class member data are usually declared private and methods public. This dichotomy is not required. It is often useful to declare one or more methods to be private. As such, these functions can only be used within the class itself; *i.e.*, they are local *utility functions*.

Example 8.5 Using private Functions gcd() and reduce()

```
class Rational {
public:
   Rational(int n=0, int d=1): num(n), den(d)
                     {reduce();}
   void print()    {cout <<num <<'/' <<den <<endl;}
private:
   int num, den;
   int gcd(int j, int k) { return k ? j: gcd(k,j%k); }
   void reduce() {int g=gcd(num,den); num/=g;
den/=g;}
};
void main() {
```

```
Rational x(100,360);
x.print();
}
```

5/18   This version includes two `private` functions. `gcd()` returns the greatest common divisor. `reduce()` uses `gcd()` to reduce the fraction `num`/`den` to lowest terms. Thus the fraction 100/360 is stored as the object 5/18.

Note!

The keywords `public` and `private` are called *access specifiers*, which specify whether the members are accessible outside the class definition. The keyword `protected` is the third access specifier. It will be described in Chapter 11.

The Copy Constructor

Every class has at least two constructors. These are identified by their unique declarations:

```
X();            // default constructor
X(const X&);    // copy constructor
```

where X is the class identifier. For example, these two special constructors for a `Widget` class would be declared:

```
Widget();                // default constructor
Widget(const Widget&);   // copy constructor
```

The first of these two special constructors is called the *default constructor;* it is called automatically whenever an object is declared in the simplest form, like this: `Widget x;`

The second of these two special constructors is called the *copy constructor;* it is called automatically whenever an object is copied *(i.e.,* duplicated), like this: `Widget y(x);`

If either of these two constructors is not defined explicitly, then it is automatically defined implicitly by the system.

The copy constructor takes one parameter: the object that it is going to copy. That object is passed by constant reference because it should not be changed. When the copy constructor is called, it copies the complete state of an existing object into a new object of the same class. If the class definition does not explicitly include a copy, then the system automatically creates one by default. The ability to write your own copy constructor gives you more control over your software.

A copy constructor for the Rational class could look like:

```
Rational(const Rational& r):
    num(r.num), den(r.den)    { }
```

The copy constructor copies the num and den fields of the parameter r into the object being constructed.

Note the required syntax for the copy constructor: it must have one parameter, which has the same class as that being declared, and it must be passed by constant reference: const X&.

You Need to Know

The copy constructor is called automatically whenever

- an object is copied by means of a declaration initialization;
- an object is passed by value to a function;
- an object is returned by value from a function.

Example 8.6 Tracing Calls to the Copy Constructor

```
class Rational {
public:
  Rational(int n, int d):num(n), den(d) { }
  Rational(const Rational& r):num(r.num), den(r.den)
    { cout <<"In COPY\n"; }
private:
  int num, den;
};
Rational f(Rational r) { // copy ? to r
  Rational s=r;         // copy r to s
  return s;             // copy s to ?
}
```

```
void main() {
  Rational x(22,7);
  Rational y(x);         // copy x to y
  f(y);
}
```

In COPY — Here, the copy constructor is called four times:
In COPY — 1. when y is declared, copying x to y
In COPY — 2. when y is passed by value to f, copying y to r
In COPY — 3. when s is declared, copying r to s;
4. when f returns, even though nothing is copied.

Note that the initialization of s looks like an assignment, but it calls the copy constructor just as the declaration of y does.

If you do not include a copy constructor in your class definition, then the "default" copy constructor will simply copy objects bit-by-bit. In many cases, this is exactly what you would want.

However, in some important cases, a bit-by-bit copy will not be adequate. The String class, defined in Chapter 10, is a prime example. In objects of that class, the relevant data member holds only a pointer to the actual string, so a bit-by-bit copy would only duplicate the pointer, not the string itself. In cases like this, it is essential that you define your own copy constructor.

When an object is created, a constructor is called to manage its birth. Similarly, when an object comes to the end of its life, another special method is called automatically to manage its death. This function is called a *destructor*.

Each class has exactly one destructor. If it is not defined explicitly, then like the default constructor, the copy constructor, and the assignment operator, the destructor is created automatically.

The class destructor is called for an object when it reaches the end of its scope. For a local object, this will be at the end of the block within which it is declared. For a static object, it will be at then end of the main() function.

Although the system will provide them automatically, it is considered good programming practice always to define the copy constructor, the assignment operator, and the destructor within each class definition.

Constant Objects

It is good programming practice to make an object constant if it should not be changed. This is done with the const keyword:

```
const char BLANK = ' ';
const int MAX_INT = 2147483647;
const double PI = 3.141592653589793;
void init(float a(), const int SIZE);
```

Like variables and function parameters, objects may also be declared to be constant: const Rational PI(22,7); When this is done, the C++ compiler restricts access to the object's methods. For example, with the Rational class defined previously, the print() function could not be called for this object:

```
PI.print();      // error: call not allowed
```

In fact, unless we modify our class definition, the only methods that could be called for const objects would be the constructors and the destructor. To overcome this restriction, we must declare as constant those methods that we want to be able to use with const objects.

A function is declared constant by inserting the const keyword between its parameter list and its body:

```
void print() const {cout <<num <<'/' <<den <<endl;}
```

This modification of the function definition will allow it to be called for constant objects:

```
const Rational PI(22,7);
PI.print();                // o.k. now
```

Structures

The C++ class is a generalization of the C `struct` (for "structure") which is a class with only public members and no functions. One normally thinks of a class as a structure that is given life by means of its methods and which enjoys information hiding by means of private data members.

To remain compatible with the older C language, C++ retains the `struct` keyword, which allows `struct`s to be defined. However, a C++ `struct` is essentially the same as a C++ `class`. The only significant difference between the two is with the default access specifier assigned to members. Although not recommended, C++ classes can be defined without explicitly specifying its member access specifier. For example,

```
class Rational { int num, den; }
```
is a valid definition of a `Rational` class. Since the access specifier for its data members `num` and `den` is not specified, it is set by default to be `private`. If we make it a `struct` instead of a `class`

```
struct Rational ( int num, den; }
```
then the data members are set by default to be `public`.

Pointers to Objects

In many applications, it is advantageous to use pointers to objects (and structs). Here is a simple example:

Example 8.7 Using Pointers to Objects

```
class X {
public:
   int data;
};
void main() {
   X* p = new X;
   (*p).data=22;   // equivalent to: p->data=22;
   cout <<"(*p).data=" <<(*p).data <<"="
        <<p->data <<endl;
   p->data=44;
```

```
cout <<"   p->data=" <<(*p).data <<"="
     <<p->data <<endl;
}
```

(*p).data=22=22
p->data=44=44

Since p is a pointer to an X object, *p is an X object, and (*p).data accesses its (public) data member data. Parentheses are required in the expression (*p).data because the direct member selection operator "." has higher precedence than the dereferencing operator "*".

The two notations: (*p).data and p->data have the same meaning. When working with pointers, the "arrow" symbol "->" is preferred as it is simpler and suggests "the thing to which p points."

Example 8.8 A Node Class for Linked Lists

This defines a Node class each of whose objects contain an int data member and a next pointer. The program allows the user to create a linked list. Then it traverses the list, printing each data value.

```
class Node {
public:
   Node(int d, Node* p=0) : data(d), next(p) { }
   int data;
   Node* next;
};
void main() {
   int n;
   Node* p;
   Node* q=0;
   while (cin >>n) {
      p = new Node(n, q);
      q = p;
   }
   for (; p->next; p=p->next)
       cout <<p->data <<" -> ";
   cout <<"*\n";
}
```

77 66 55 44 33 22^D
22 -> 33 -> 44 -> 55 -> 66 -> 77 -> *

First note that the definition of the Node class includes two references to the class itself. This is allowed because each reference is actually a pointer to the class. Also, note that the constructor initializes both data members.

The `while` loop continues reading `int`s into n until the user enters the end-of-file character. Within the loop, it gets a new node, inserts the `int` into its data member, and connects the new node to the previous node (pointed to by q). Then, the `for` loop traverses the list. It starts with the node pointed to by p (the last node constructed) and continues until p->next is NUL (last node in the list).

static Data Members

Sometimes a value is needed by all members of the class. It would be inefficient to store this value in every object of the class so we declare the data member to be `static` by including the `static` keyword at the beginning of the variable's declaration. It also requires that the variable be defined globally. The syntax looks like this:

```
class X {
public:
    static int n; // declare n a static data member
};
int X::n = 0;     // definition of n
```

> Static variables are automatically initialized to 0, so the explicit initialization is unnecessary unless you need a nonzero initial value.

Example 8.9 A static Data Member

```
class Widget {
public:
    Widget() { ++count; }
    ~Widget() { −count; }
    static int count
};
```

The `Widget` class maintains a `static` data member count, which keeps track of the number of `Widget` objects in existence. Each time a widget is created the counter is incremented, and

```
int Widget :: count = 0;
void main()   {
   Widget w, x;
   cout <<w.count <<" widgets.\n";
   { Widget w, x, y, z;
     cout <<w.count <<" widgets.\n";
   }
   cout <<w.count <<" widgets.\n";
   Widget y;
   cout <<w.count <<" widgets.\n";
}
```

each time a widget is destroyed the counter is decremented.

```
2 widgets.
6 widgets.
2 widgets.
3 widgets.
```

Notice how four widgets are created in the inner block, and then destroyed when program control leaves that block, reducing the global number of widgets from 6 to 2.

A static data member is like an ordinary global variable: only one copy of the variable exists no matter how many instances of the class exist. The main difference is that it is a data member of the class, and so may be private. If we made the static variable count private, we would need an access function like numWidgets() to obtain the value in the main program:

```
int numWidgets() { return count; }
```

static Function Members

Like most methods, numWidgets() requires that it be owned by some instance of the class. But it returns the value of the static data member count that is independent of the individual objects themselves. Since the action of the function is independent of the actual function objects, it would make sense to have the calls independent of them too. This can be done by declaring the function to be static.

Example 8.10 A static Function Member
The Widget class maintains a static data member count, which keeps track of the number of Widget objects in existence globally.

```
class Widget {
public:
   Widget() { ++count; }
```

```
    ~Widget() { —count; }
    static int num() { return count; }
private:
    static int count;
};
```

Declaring the num() function to be static renders it independent of the class instances. So now it is invoked simply as a member of the Widget class using the scope resolution operator ": :".

```
            cout <<Widget::num() <<" widgets.\n";
```

This allows the function to be called before any objects have been instantiated.

Now the method num() has no "this" pointer. As a static method, it is associated with the class itself, not with its instances. Static methods can access only static data from their own class.

Chapter 9
OVERLOADING OPERATORS

113

C++ includes a rich store of operators that are defined automatically for fundamental types (int, float, *etc.*). When you create a new type (class) you can overload most C++ operators to this user-defined type.

Overloading the Assignment Operator

Of all the operators, the assignment operator = is probably used the most. Its purpose is to copy one object to another. Like the default constructor, the copy constructor, and the destructor, the assignment operator is created automatically for every class that is defined, but it can be defined explicitly in the class definition.

Example 9.1 An Assignment Operator for the Rational Class

Rational default and copy constructors and assignment operator:

```
class Rational {
public:
  Rational(int =0, int =1);   // default const
  Rational(const Rational&); // copy constructor
  void operator=(const Rational&); // assignment
  // other declarations go here
private:
  int num, den;
};
```

The name of this member function is operator=. Its argument list is the same as that of the copy constructor: it contains a single argument of the same class, passed by constant reference.

Here is the implementation of the overloaded assignment operator:

```
void Rational::operator=(const Rational& r) {
  num=r.num;   den=r.den;   }
```

It copies the member data from r to the object that owns the call.

The this Pointer

C++ allows assignments to be chained together, like this:

```
x = y = z = 3.14;
```

This is executed first by assigning 3.14 to z, then to y, and finally to x.

As Ex. 9.1 shows, the assignment operator is really a function named `operator=`. In this chain, the function is called three times nested, like this: `f(x, f(y, f(z, 3.14)))`

As assignment operator returns the value it assigns, it should return a reference to the same type as the object being assigned:

```
Rational& operator=(Rational& r)
```

This allows assignments to be chained together.

Example 9.2 Preferred Prototype for an Overloaded Assignment

```
// assignment
Rational& operator = (const Rational&);
```

The function should return the object that is being assigned, in order for the assignment chain to work. Since there is no other name available for this owner object, C++ defines a special pointer, named `this`, which points to the owner object. Using the `this` pointer we can give the correct implementation of the overloaded assignment operator:

Example 9.3 Implementation of the `Rational` Class Assignment

```
Rational& Rational::operator = (const Rational& r) {
  num = r.num;   den = r.den;
  return *this;
}
```

Now assignments for the `Rational` class can be chained together:

```
Rational x, y, z(22,7);     x = y = z;
```

Finally, note that an assignment is different from an initialization, even though they both use the equals sign:

```
Rational x(22,7); // this is an initialization
Rational y(x);    // this is an initialization
Rational z = x;   // this is an initialization
Rational w;
w = x;                 // this is an assignment
```

An initialization calls the copy constructor. An assignment calls the assignment operator.

Overloading Arithmetic Operators

Most programming languages provide the standard arithmetic operators +, -, *, and / for numeric types. Therefore, it is natural to define these for user-defined types like the `Rational` class. In older programming languages, this is done by defining functions like this:

```
Rational product(Rational x, Rational y) {
    Rational z(x.num*y.num, x.den*y.den);
    return z;   }
```

This works, but the function has to be called in the conventional way:

```
z = product(x,y);
```

C++ allows such functions to be defined using the standard arithmetic operator symbols, so that they can be called more naturally using infix notation (e.g., `z = x*y;`). Like most operators in C++, the multiplication operator has a function name: `operator*`. Using this in place of "product" in the code above results in

```
Rational operator*(Rational x, Rational y) {
    Rational z(x.num*y.num, x.den*y.den);
    return z;   }
```

However, this is not a member function of `Rational`. Since the overloaded arithmetic operators cannot be member functions, they cannot access the `private` member data `num` and `den`. Fortunately, C++ allows an exception to this by allowing us to declare the function as *a friend* of the Rational class.

Note!

A `friend` function is a nonmember function that is given access to all members of the class within which it is declared. `friends` have all the privileges of member functions without actually being a class member. This attribute is used mostly with overloaded operators.

Example 9.4 Making the Multiplication Operator a `friend`

Here a `friend` function overloads the multiplication operator:

```
class Rational {
    friend Rational operator*
                (const Rational&, const Rational&);
public:
    Rational(int =0, int =1);
    Rational(const Rational&);
```

```
Rational& operator=(const Rational&);
// other declarations go here
private:
  int num;
  int den;
  // other declarations go here
};
```

The function prototype is inserted in the class declaration, above the
public section and the arguments are passed by constant reference.

Now we can implement this nonmember just as we had expected:

```
Rational operator*
    (const Rational& x, const Rational& y) {
  Rational z(x.num*y.num, x.den*y.den);
  return z;
}
```

Note that the keyword friend is not used in the function implementation. Also note that the scope resolution prefix Rational:: is not used
because this is not a member function.

Here is a little program that uses our improved Rational class:

Example 9.5 Rational with Assignment and Multiplication

```
Rational x(22,7), y(-3,8), z;
z = x;        // assignment operator called
z.print();   cout <<endl;
x = y*z;     // multiplication operator called
x.print();   cout <<endl;
```

The reduce() function would be called from within the overloaded
multiplication operator to reduce -66/56 to -33/28.

Overloading the Arithmetic Assignment Operators

C++ allows you to combine arithmetic operations with the assignment
operator: for example, using x*=y in place of x=x*y. All combination
operators can be overloaded for use in your own classes.

Example 9.6 The Rational Class with an Overloaded *=

```
Rational& Rational::operator* = (const Rational& r) {
  num=num*r.num;     den=den*r.den;
```

```
    return *this;
}
```

The operator `operator*=` has the same syntax and nearly the same implementation as the basic assignment operator `operator=`. By returning *this, the operator can be chained (x *= y *= z;)

It is also important to ensure that overloaded operators perform consistently with each other. For example, (x=x*y;) and (x*=y;) should have the same effect, even though they call different operators.

Overloading the Relational Operators

The relational operators <, >, <=, >=, ==, and != can be also be overloaded as `friend` functions.

Example 9.7 Overloading the Rational Equality Operator ==

Like other `friend`s, the == operator is declared above the `public` section of the class:

```
    class Rational {
       friend int operator ==
               (const Rational&, const Rational&);
       // other declarations go here
    public:
       // other declarations go here
    private:
       int num, den;
       // other declarations go here
    };
    int operator ==
               (const Rational& x, const Rational& y) {
          return (x.num*y.den == y.num*x.den);
    }
```

The test for equality of two fractions *a/b* and *c/d* is equivalent to the test *ad* == *bc*. So we end up using the equality operator for `int`s to define the equality operator for `Rational`s.

Overloading the Stream Operators

C++ allows you to overload the stream operators >> and << to customize input and output. Like the arithmetic and relational operators, these should also be declared as `friend` functions.

For a class T with data member d, the syntax for the << operator is

```
friend ostream& operator<<(ostream& os, const T& t)
    return os <<t.d; }
```

ostream is a standard class defined in the <iostream.h>. The parameters and the return value are passed by reference. This function can then be called using the syntax used for fundamental types:

```
cout <<"x = " <<x <<", y = " <<y <<endl;
```

Example 9.8 Overloading the `Rational` Output Operator <<

```
class Rational {
  friend ostream& operator<<
      (ostream&, const Rational&);
public:
  Rational(int n=0, int d=1) : num(n), den(d) { }
  // other declarations go here
private:
  int num, den;
  // other declarations go here
};
void main() {
  Rational x(22,7), y(-3,8);
  cout <<"x=" <<x <<", y=" <<y <<endl;
}
ostream& operator<<(ostream& os, const Rational& r)
{
  return os <<r.num <<'/' <<r.den; }
```

`x=22/7, y=-3/8` When the second line of main() executes, the expression cout <<"x = " executes first. This calls the standard output operator <<, passing the standard output stream cout and the string "x=" to it. As usual, this inserts the string into the output stream and returns a reference to cout. This return value is then passed with the object x to the overloaded << operator. This call to operator << executes with cout in place of os and with x in place of r. The result is the execution of the line: `return  os  <<r.num  <<'/'` `<<r.den;` which inserts 22/7 into the output stream and returns a reference to `cout`. Then another call to the standard output operator `<<` and another call to the overloaded operator are made, with the output (a reference to `cout`) of each call cascading into the next call as input. Finally the last call to operator `<<` is made, passing `cout` and `endl`. This flushes the stream, causing the line x=22/7, y=-3/8 to be printed.

The syntax for overloading `>>` is similar to `<<`. Here, `istream` is another standard class defined in the `iostream.h` header file. Here is an example of how custom input can be written:

Example 9.9 Overloading the `Rational` Input Operator `>>`

```
istream& operator>>(istream& is, Rational& r) {
    cout <<"\t  Numerator: ";     is >>r.num;
    cout <<"\tDenominator: ";     is >>r.den;
    r.reduce();
    return is;
}
```

This version of the input operator includes user prompts to facilitate input. It also includes a call to the utility function `reduce()`. Note that, as a `friend`, the operator can access this private function.

Conversion Operators

In our original implementation of `Rational` we defined the member function `convert()` to convert from `Rational` to `double`:

```
double convert() {return double(num)/den;}
```

This requires the member function to be called as

```
x.convert();
```

In keeping with our goal to make objects of the `Rational` class behave like objects of fundamental types, we will build a conversion function that can be called the same way as ordinary type conversions:

```
n = int(t);
y = double(x);
```

This can be done with a conversion operator.

Our `Rational` class already has the facility to convert an object from `int` to `Rational`. (Rational x(22);) is handled by the default constructor, which assigns 22 to `x.num` and 1 to `x.den`. This constructor also handles direct type conversions from type `int` to type `Rational` by `x = Rational(22);`. Constructors of a given class are used to convert from another type to that class type.

To convert from the given class type to another type requires a different kind of member function. It is called a *conversion operator,* and it has a different syntax. If `type` is the type to which the object is to be converted, then the conversion operator is declared as

```
operator tvpe();
```
For example, a member function of the `Rational` class that returns an equivalent `float` would be declared as: `operator float();`.

If we want to convert to type `double`, we would declare it as: `operator double();`. If we want it usable for constant `Rationals` (like pi), then we would declare it as: `operator double() const;`. Recall that, in our original implementation of the `Rational` class we defined the member function `convert()` for this purpose.

Example 9.10 Adding a Conversion Operator to the `Rational` Class

```
Rational::operator double() const {
   return double(num)/den;
}
```
Consider the following code fragment:

```
Rational x(-5,8);
cout <<"x=" <<x <<", x=" <<double(x) <<endl;
const Rational p(22,7);
const double pi = double(p);
cout <<"p=" <<p <<", pi=" <<pi <<endl;
```
First we use the conversion operator `double()` to convert the `Rational` object x into the `double` -0.625. Then we use it again to convert the constant `Rational` object p into the constant `double` pi.

Overloading the Increment and Decrement Operators

The increment operator ++ and the decrement operator – each have two forms: prefix and postfix. Each of these four forms can be overloaded.

We'll examine the overloading of the increment operator here. Overloading the decrement operator works the same way.

When applied to integer types, the pre-increment operator adds 1 to the value of the object being incremented. This is a unary operator: its single argument is the object being incremented. The syntax for overloading it for a class named `T` is simply `T operator++();` so for our `Rational` class, it is declared as `Rational operator++ ();`

Example 9.11 A Pre-Increment Operator for the `Rational` Class

This example adds a `Rational` pre-increment operator `++` to our class. Although we can make this function do whatever we want, it should be consistent with the action that the standard pre-increment operator performs on integer types. That adds 1 to the value of the object <u>before</u> that value is used in the expression. This is equivalent to adding its denominator to its numerator, so we simply add `den` to `num` and then return `*this`, which is the object itself.

```
Rational Rational::operator++() { //pre ++
   num += den;
   return *this;
}
```

Postfix operators have the same function name as the prefix operators. For example, both the pre-increment and the post-increment operator are named `operator++`. To distinguish them, C++ specifies that the prefix operator has one argument and the postfix operator has two arguments. (When used, they both appear to have one argument.) So the correct syntax for the prototype for an overloaded post-increment operator is `T operator++ (int);`

Example 9.12 Adding a `Rational` Post-Increment Operator

To be consistent with the ordinary post-increment operator for integer types, this overloaded version should not change the value of x until after it has been assigned to y. To do that, we need a temporary object

The required argument must have type `int`. This appears a bit strange because no integer is passed to the function when it is invoked. The integer argument is thus a *dummy argument,* required only so that the postfix operator can be distinguished from the prefix operator.

to hold the contents of the object that owns the call. This is done by assigning *this to temp. Then this object can be returned after adding den to num.

```
Rational Rational::operator++(int) { // post ++
   Rational temp = *this;
   num += den;
   return temp;
}
```

Note that the dummy argument in the operator++ function is an unnamed int. It need not be named because it is not used. But it must be declared to distinguish the post-increment from the pre-increment operator.

Overloading the Subscript Operator

If a is an array, then the expression a[i] really is the same as *(a + i). This is because a is actually the address of the initial element in the array, so a + i is the address of the ith element, since the number of bytes added to a is i times the size of each array element

The symbol [] denotes the *subscript operator*. Its name derives from the original use of arrays, where a[i] represented the mathematical symbol a_i. When used as a[i], it has two operands: a and i. The expression a[i] is equivalent to operator [](a, i). And as an operator, [] can be overloaded.

Example 9.13 Adding a Rational Subscript Operator

```
#include <stdlib.h>     // defines exit() function
int& Rational::operator[](int i) {
   if (i == 1) return num;
   if (i == 2) return den;
   cerr <<"ERROR: index out of range\n";
   exit(0);
}
```

An expression x[1] would call the subscript operator, passing 1 to i, which returns x.num. Similarly, x[2] would return x.den. If i has any value other than 1 or 2, then an error message is sent to cerr, the standard error stream, and then the exit() function is called.

This example is artificial in that there is no advantage to accessing the fields of the `Rational` object x with x[1] and x[2] instead of x.num and x.den. However, there are many important classes where the subscript is very useful.

> Note that the subscript operator is an access function, since it provides `public` access to `private` member data.

Chapter 10
A STRING CLASS

Chapter 7 described the way that character strings are handled using C-style programming: each string is implemented as a pointer `p` to a `char` in memory. The actual string of characters that `p` represents are held in a contiguous block beginning with byte `*p` and terminated with the NUL character. To distinguish this representation from that to be defined in this chapter, we will refer to the former as "C-strings."

Chapter 7 also described the `string.h` header file. It defines many functions that operate on C-strings. The `String` class will include functions that perform equivalent operations on `String` objects and of these new operations will be implemented using functions from the `string.h` header file.

The character string abstract data type is an ideal candidate for implementation as a C++ class, encapsulating the data and functionality in individualized objects. This chapter shows one way to do that. Such an implementation allows us to use objects of a `String` class.

The `String` Class Interface

There are generally two methods for delimiting an un-indexed sequence of objects. One method is to use a distinguished object to signal the end of the sequence (e.g., the NUL in C-strings). Another method is to store the length of the sequence with the sequence. This is how we will implement our `String` class:

```
unsigned len;   // number of (non-NUL) characters
char* buf;      // actual character string
```

Here, `len` will be the length of the sequence of characters and `buf` (a C-string) will be the "buffer" that holds them.

For example, suppose that `name` is a `String` object representing the C-string "Natalie B." Then we can visualize it like this:

This implementation will improve the efficiency of some string operations. For example, to determine that "Shaum's Outline" and "Shaum's Outline!" are not equal requires examining all 31 characters. But since we are storing the strings' lengths in our `String` class, the comparison operator need only compare the integers 15 and 16 to determine that these two strings are not equal.

Here is the class interface for a `String` class:

```
#include <iostream.h>
class String {
  friend int operator==(const String&, const String&);
  friend int operator!=(const String&, const String&);
  friend int operator<(const String&, const String&);
  friend int operator<=(const String&, const String&);
  friend int operator>(const String&, const String&);
  friend int operator>=(const String&, const String&);
  friend ostream& operator<<(ostream&, const String&);
  friend istream& operator>>(istrealn&, String&);
  friend String operator+(const String&, const String&);
public:
  String(unsigned =0);      // default constructor
  String(char, unsigned); // constructor
  String(const char*);      // constructor
  String(const String&);    // copy constructor
  ~String();                // destructor
  String& operator=(const String&);  // assignment
  String& operator+=(const String&); // append
  operator char*() const;            // converstion
  char& operator[] (unsigned) const; // subscript
  unsigned length() const;           // access method
private:
  unsigned len;   // number of non-null characters
  char* buf;      // actual character string
}
```

The Constructors and Destructor

Here is the implementation of the three constructors. The first constructs
a `String` object containing n blanks. If no parameter is passed, then
n becomes the default 0 and the null string is constructed.

```
String::String(unsigned n) : len(n) {
  buf = new char[len+1];
```

```
        for (int i=0; i<len; i++) buf[i]=' ';
        buf[len] = '\0';
    }
```

The second constructor creates a string of identical characters.

```
    String::String(char c, unsigned n) : len(n) {
        buf = new char[len+1];
        for (int i=0; i<len; i++) buf[i] = c;
        buf[len] = '\0';
    }
```

The third constructor converts a C-string into a String object.

```
    String::String(const char* s) {
        len = strlen(s)
        buf = new char[len+1];
        for (int i=0; i<len; i++) buf[i] =s[i];
        buf[len] = '\n';
    }
```

Example 10.1 Testing the Constructor

The code invokes the default constructor twice: once with no parameter and once with length 4. It invokes the second constructor with 4 B's, and the third with with a string.

```
    String s1, s2(4), s3('B', 4), s4("Hello, World!");
    cout <<"s1 = [" <<s1 <<"], len=" <<s1.length();
    cout <<"       s2 = [" <<s2 <<"], len="
        <<s2.length() <<endl;
    cout <<"s3 = [" <<s3 <<"], len=" <<s3.length();
    cout <<"    s4 = [" <<s4 <<"], len="
        <<s4.length() <<endl;
```

```
s1 = [], len=0          s2 = [    ], len=4
s3 = [BBBB], len=4      s4 = [Hello, World!], len=13
```

The destructor for our String class is typical:

```
        String::~String() { delete [] buf; }
```

It uses the `delete` operator to release the object's memory. The subscript operator `[]` must be specified because `buf` is an array.

The Copy Constructor

In many class definitions, instead of defining a copy constructor explicitly, we use the default which does a direct copy of each corresponding data member. This doesn't work for our String class because a direct memory copy would duplicate the buf pointer but not the string to which it points. This would yield two different objects with the same data. So, we define our own copy constructor:

```
String::String(const String& s):len(s.len) {
  buf = new char[len+1];
  for (int i=0; i<s.len; i++) buf[i]=s.buf[i];
    buf[len]='\0';
}
```

This works the same way as the third constructor, except that the string it duplicates is an existing String object instead of a C-string. Also, we can use an initialization list to assign s.len to the new object's len field. That was not possible in the third constructor because we had to invoke a function (strlen()) to obtain the length of s.

Example l0.2 Testing the Copy Constructor
This test invokes the copy constructor twice: once when it initializes the object self, and once when it initializes the object sis:

```
#include "String.h"
void main() {
  String me("Jennifer");
  cout <<"me = [" <<name <<"]\n";
  String self = me;            // calls copy constructor
  cout <<"self = [" <<self <<"]\n";
  String sis = "Natalie B.";  // calls 2 constructors
  cout <<"sis = [" <<sis <<"]\n";
}
```

```
me = [Jennifer]
self = [Jennifer]
sis = [Natalie B.]
```

First it uses the third constructor to construct the String object me which duplicates the constant C-string "Jennifer." Then it uses the copy constructor to create the String object self that duplicates the String object me by being initialized by it. The last declaration uses both constructors to construct the String object sis. First it uses the third constructor to create a temporary String object that duplicates the constant C-string "Natalie B." Then it uses the copy constructor to create the String object sis to duplicate the temporary object.

The Assignment Operator

The assignment operator is used whenever one object is assigned to another object that has already been declared of the same class. Like the copy constructor, the assignment operator is automatically provided by the compiler if we don't write our own version.

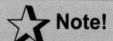 **Note!**

It is unwise to rely upon the automatically generated assignment operator for classes whose objects contain pointers, because duplicating pointers does not duplicate the data to which they point.

Example 10.3 Using the Compiler Default Assignment Operator
This example shows what can go wrong when you rely upon the automatically generated assignment operator for the String class:

```
String myCar = "Infiniti G20";
String yourCar = "Lexus ES300";
cout <<"\t   myCar = [" <<myCar <<"]\n";
cout <<"\tyourCar = [" <<yourCar <<"]\n";
myCar = yourCar;          // memberwise assignment
cout <<"After: myCar = yourCar\n";
cout <<"\t   myCar = [" <<myCar <<"]\n";
cout <<"\tyourCar = [" <<yourCar <<"]\n";
yourCar[6] = 'L';
cout <<"After: yourCar[6] = 'L'\n";
cout <<" MyCar = [" <<myCar <<"]\n";
cout <<" yourCar = [" <<yourCar <<"]\n";
```

```
MyCar = [Infiniti G20]
yourCar = [Lexus ES300]
After: myCar = yourCar
MyCar = [Lexus ES300]
yourCar = [Lexus ES300]
After: yourCar[6] = 'L'
MyCar = [Lexus LS300]
yourCar = [Lexus LS300]
```

The default assignment operator uses "member-wise assignment." For our `String` class, that means that in the fifth statement in `main()`, `yourCar.len` is assigned to `myCar.len` and `yourCar.buf` is assigned to `myCar.buf`. But the `buf` members are pointers, so the result is that both `yourCar.buf` and `myCar.buf` point to the same C-string in memory: the one that contains "Lexus ES300." So when you buy a new Lexus LS3OO, it becomes my car too! In other words, the assignment `myCar = yourCar` in this program means that I become a co-owner of your new Lexus LS3OO (and that I lost my Lexus ES3OO).

Both objects, `yourCar` and `myCar`, point to the same character string in memory. The assignment `myCar = yourCar` simply duplicated the integer `len` and the pointer `buf`, without duplicating the character string. So when the "E" is changed to an "L," it gets changed in both objects. To overcome this problem, we need to define our own assignment operator so that an assignment `y = x` replaces the object `y` with a duplicate of the object `x`.

Here is our own assignment operator, defined explicitly:

```
String& String: operator (const String& s) {
    if (&s == this) return *this;
    len = s.len;
    delete [] buf;
    buf = new char[s.len + 1];
    strcpy(buf, s.buf);
    return *this;
}
```

First, it checks whether the object `s` is different from the object to which it is to be assigned. If they are the same object, then nothing more needs to be done. If the two objects are not the same, then we recreate the current object so that it becomes a duplicate of `s`. After setting `len` to `s.len`, we deallocate the memory currently assigned to `buf` and then allocate a new string of bytes of the correct length (`s.len+1`). Then we use the `strcpy()` function (defined in `string.h`) to copy `s.buf` into `buf` and return `*this`.

The Addition Operator

The addition operator + is a natural choice for the concatenation function in a String class. After all, concatenation means adding two strings together to form a new string.

Here is the concatenation function for our String class:

```
String operator+(const const String& s1, const String& s2) {
    string s(s1.len + s2.len);
    strcpy(s.buf, s1.buf);
    strcat(s.buf, s2.buf);
    return s;
}
```

First, it constructs a String object s of length s1.len+s2.len. Then it uses the strcpy() and strcat() (in <string.h>) to copy s1.buf to s.buf and append s2.buf to it.

An Append Operator

The += operator is one of a series of arithmetic assignment operators that combine the arithmetic operators (+, -, *, *etc.)* with the assignment operator.

Don't Forget!

Like most operators, the arithmetic assignment operators can be overloaded to perform whatever operations you want. However, it is unwise to define an overloaded operator to do anything that is not similar to the action of the original operator.

Here is the overloaded `+=` operator for our `String` class:

```
String& String::operator+=(const String& s) {
    len += s.len;
    char* tempbuf = new char[len+1];
    strcpy(tempbuf, buf);    strcat(tempbuf, s.buf);
    delete [] buf;
    buf = tempbuf;
    return *this;
}
```

First it increments its `len` field by the length of the `String` object passed to it. Then it allocates the total number of bytes needed for the new string and holds this space in the temporary C-string `tempbuf`. Then, it uses the `strcpy()` and `strcat()` to copy its `buf` to `tempbuf` and then append `s.buf` to it. Now it can release the memory allocated to its original buffer and then assign the `tempbuf` pointer to it.

Example 10.4 Testing the += Operator
This test driver invokes the `+=` operator to append the string `", Jr."` to the `String` object `name`.

```
#include "String.h"
int main() {
    String name("Bob Brown");
    cout <<"name = [" <<name <<"]\n";
    name += ", Jr.";
    cout <<"name = [" <<name <<"]\n";
}
```

```
name = [Bob Brown]
name = [Bob Brown, Jr.]
```

The third constructor is invoked to convert the C-string `String` object before it is passed to the `+=` operator.

Access Functions — The * Operator

`operator char*() const;` is a conversion operator that converts a `String` object into a C-string. It has the reverse effect of the constructor: `String (const char*);` which converts a C-string into a `String` object.

This conversion operator has a very simple implementation:

```
String::operator char*() const {    return buf;}
```

Its `buf` data member is the C-string that we want. This conversion operator is an access function: it simply provides public access to the private data member `buf`. It is not really an "inverse" of the `String (const char*)` constructor because it does not create a new C-string. As an access function, it merely provides public access to the `buf` C-string that already exists within the `String` object.

Example 10.5 Testing the Conversion to C-String Operator

```
String name("Bethany");    // a String object
cout <<"name = [" <<name <<"]\n";
char* s = name;            // s is a C-string
cout <<"s = [" <<s <<"]\n";
```

Here is the overloaded subscript operator for our `String` class:

```
char& String::operator[](unsigned i) const
                              { return buf[i]; }
```

It simply returns the *i*th element of the object's buf buffer.

Example 10.6 Testing the Subscript Operator

```
String name("C. Babbage");
cout <<"name=[" <<name <<"]\n";
cout <<"name[3]=[" <<name[3] <<"]\n";
name[3] = 'C';
cout <<"name[3]=[" <<name[3] <<"]\n";
cout <<"name=[" <<name <<"]\n";
```

```
name=[C. Babbage]
name[3] = [B]
name[3] = [C]
name=[C. Cabbage]
```

The only surprising result here is that the expression `name[8]`, which invokes the function, can be used on the left side of an assignment! This works because the expression is an *lvalue*.

The other access function in `String` is the `length()` function:

```
unsigned String::length() const { return len; }
```

We have already tested the `length()` function in Ex. 10.1.

The Comparison Operators

We now overload all six of the comparison operators: ==, !=, <, <=, >, and >=. Since all are defined for C-strings in <string.h>, their implementation for our `String` class is trivial and three are shown here:

```
int operator==(const String& s1, const String& s2) {
    return (strcmp(s1.buf, s2.buf) == 0); }
int operator!=(const String& s1, const String& s2) {
    return (strcmp(s1.buf, s2.buf) != 0); }
int operator<(const String& si, const String& s2) {
    return (strcmp(s1.buf, s2.buf) < 0); }
```

All simply call the `strcmp()`. It returns an integer whose sign indicates how the two *C-strings* compare: negative *means* that the first C-string lexicographically precedes the second; zero means that the two are equal; and positive means that the first lexicographically follows the second.

Example 10.7 Testing the Comparison Operators

```
String x, y;
cout <<"Enter two strings: ";
cin >>x >>y; cout <<'\n';
if (x==y) cout <<"   ["  <<x <<"]==["  <<y <<"]";
if (x!=y) cout <<"   ["  <<x <<"]!=["  <<y <<"]";
if (x< y) cout <<"   ["  <<x <<"]<["  <<y <<"]";
if (x<=y) cout <<"   ["  <<x <<"]<=["  <<y <<"]";
if (x> y) cout <<"   ["  <<x <<"]>["  <<y <<"]";
if (x>=y) cout <<"   ["  <<x <<"]>=["  <<y <<"]";
```

```
Enter two strings: ABC AB
   [ABC]!=[AB]   [ABC]>[AB]   [ABC]>=[AB]
```

Stream Operators

The stream operators overloaded for our `String` class are the stream insertion operator `<<` and the stream extraction operator `>>`. We have already used these in several test drivers. Here are their implementations:

```
ostream& operator<<(ostream& ostr, const String& s)
{   return ostr <<s.buf;   }
istream& operator>>(istream& istr, String& s) {
    char buffer[256];
    istr >>buffer;
    s = buffer;
    return istr; }
```

The overloaded stream insertion operator `<<` inserts the object's `buf` into the output stream `ostr` and then returns that reference. The overloaded stream extraction operator `>>` uses a temporary `buffer` string to read the input, assigns it to the reference `s`, and then returns the `istream` reference `istr`.

Note that both of these overloaded stream operators return the stream object that is passed to them. This makes these functions consistent with the corresponding predefined stream operators, allowing them to be invoked in cascades like this.

Example 10.8 Testing the Stream Operators

```
String s1, s2;
cin >>s1 >>s2;
cout <<s1 <<"####" <<s2 <<endl;
```

```
Hello, World!
Hello,####World!
```

The first call is `operator>>(cin, s1)` which passes a reference to the `istream` object `cin` to the parameter `istr` and a reference to the `String` object `s1` to the parameter `s`. Then `"Hello,"` is read into the C-string `temp`. This is assigned to the `String` object `s1`, and then a reference to `cin` is returned. That return value is then used in the second call `operator>>(cin, s2)` which works the same way, leaving the object `s2` representing `"World!"`.

The output line intermingles the two calls to the overloaded `<<`operator with the two calls to the standard `<<`operator in the cascade: `f(f(f(f(cout, s1), "####"), s2 ), endl );` where f is operator `<<`.

Chapter 11

COMPOSITION AND INHERITANCE

IN THIS CHAPTER:

- ✔ *Composition*
- ✔ *Inheritance*
- ✔ `protected` *Class Members*
- ✔ *Overriding and Dominating Inherited Members*
- ✔ `private` *Access versus* `protected` *Access*
- ✔ `virtual` *Functions and Polymorphism*
- ✔ *Virtual Destructors*

We often use existing classes to define new classes. The two ways to do this are called *composition* and the *inheritance*. This chapter describes both methods.

Composition

Composition of classes refers to the use of one or more classes within the definition of another class. When a data member of the new class is an object of another class, we say that the new class is a *composite* of the other objects.

Example 11.1 A `Person` Class
Here is a simple definition for a class to represent people.

```
#include "String.h"
class Person {
public:
    Person(char* n="", char* c="", int s=1)
        : name(n), city(c), sex(s) { }
    void printName() {cout <<name;}
    void printCity() {cout <<city;}
private:
    String name, city;
    int sex;
};
void main() {
    Person satchmo("Louis Armstrong", "New Orleans");
    satchmo.printName();
    cout <<"/nBorn in ";
    satchmo.printCity();
    cout <<".\n";
}
```

```
Louis Armstrong
Born in New Orleans
```

We have used the `String` class (Chap. 10) to declare the data members `name` and `city` for the `Person` class. Notice that we used the `String` overloaded insertion operator `<<` in the `Person` class's `printName()` function.

Example 11.1 illustrates the *composition* of the `String` class within the `Person` class. The next example defines another class that we can compose with this class to improve it:

Example 11.2 A `Date` Class

```
class Date {
    friend istream& operator>>(istream&, Date&);
    friend ostream& operator<<(ostream&, const Date&);
```

```
public:
  Date(int m=0, int d=0, int y=0):
        month(m), day(d), year(y) { }
  void setDate(int m, int d, int y)
       { month=m; day=d; year=y; }
private:
  int month, day, year;
};
istream& operator>>(istream& in, Date& x) {
  in >>x.month >>x.day >>x.year;
  return in;
}
ostream& operator<<(ostream& out, const Date& x) {
    static char* monthName[13]={ "", "Jan",
      "Feb", "Mar", "Apr", "May", "Jun", "Jul",
      "Aug", "Sep", "Oct", "Nov", "Dec" };
    out <<monthName[x.month] <<' ' <<x.day <<", "
       <<x.year;
    return out;
}
void main() {
  Date peace(11,11,1918);
  cout <<"WW I ended on " <<peace <<".\n";
  peace.setDate(8,14,1945);
  cout <<"WW II ended on " <<peace <<".\n";
  cout <<"Enter mth, day, & yr: ";
  Date date;
  cin >>date;
  cout <<"The date is " <<date <<".\n";
}
```

```
WW I ended on Nov 11, 1918
WW II ended on Aug 14, 1945
Enter mth, day, & yr: 7 4 1776
The date is Jul 4, 1776
```

The test driver tests the default constructor, the `setDate()` function, the overloaded `<<`, and the overloaded `>>`. Now we can use the `Date` class inside the `Person` class to store a person's date of birth.

Example 11.3 Composing `Date` Class with `Person` Class

```
#include "String.h"
#include "Date.h"
class Person {
public:
  void setDOB(int m, int d, int y)
       { dob.setDate(m, d, y); }
  void setDOD(int m, int d, int y)
       { dod.setDate(m, d, y); }
  // other methods as in in Ex. 11.1
private:
  Date dob, dod;          // dates of birth & death
};
```

```
  satchmo.setDOB(7,4,1900);
  satchmo.setDOD(8,15,1971);
  satchmo.printName();
  cout <<"\nBorn on ";   satchmo.printDOB();
  cout <<"\nDied on ";   satchmo.printDOD();
  cout <<".\n";
```

```
Louis Armstrong
Born on July 4, 1900
```

Notice again that we have used a method of one class to define methods of the composed class: the `setDate()` function is used to define the `setDOB()` function.

Composition is one way of reusing software to create new software.

Inheritance

Another way to reuse software is by means of inheritance (also called specialization or derivation). The common syntax for deriving a class Y from a class X is

```
    class Y : public X {
    // . . .
    };
```

Here X is called the *base class* (or *superclass*) and Y is called the *derived class* (or *subclass*). The keyword `public` after the colon specifies *public inheritance*, which means that `public` members of the base class become `public` members of the derived class.

Example 11.4 Deriving a `Student` Class from the `Person` Class

Since students are people it is natural to use the `Person` class to derive a `Student` class:

```
#include "Person.h"
class Student : public Person {
public:
   Student(char* n, int s=0, char* i=""):
         Person(n, s), id(i), credits(0) { }
   void setDOE(int m, int d, int y)
         { dom.setDate(m, d, y); }
   void printDOE() { cout <<dom; }
private:
   String id;        // student identification number
   Date doe;         // date entered college
   int credits;      // course credits
   float gpa;        // grade-point average
};
```

The `Student` class inherits all the `public` methods of the `Person` class, including its `constructor`. `Student` uses `Person`'s to initialize the `Person` class name. Since this is a `private` member of the `Person` class it could not be accessed directly.

Here is a test driver for the `Student` class:

```
   Student x("Ann Jones", "219360061");
   x.setDOB(7, 10, 1983);
   x.setDOE(8, 26, 2001);
   x.printName();
   cout <<"\n    Born: "; x.printDOB();
   cout <<"\nEntered: "; x.printDOE(); cout <<endl;
```

```
Beth Jones
     Born: Jul 10, 1983
Entered: Aug 26, 2001
```

Remember!

Inheritance is also call "specialization" or "derivation."

protected Class Members

The Student class in Ex. 11.4 has a significant problem: it cannot directly access the private data members of its Person superclass: name, city, DOB, DOD, and sex. The lack of access of the first four of these are not serious because these can be written and read through the Person class' constructor and public access functions. However, there is no way to write or read a Student's sex. One way to overcome this problem would be to make sex a data member of the Student class. But that is unnatural: sex is an attribute that all Person objects have, not just Students. A better solution is to change the private access specifier to protected in the Person class. That will allow access to these data members from derived classes.

Example 11.5 The Person Class with protected Data Members
Change the private access specifier of Ex. 11.3 and 11.4 to protected and add the method printSex() to the Student class:

```
class Person {
public:
    .
    .
protected:
    String name, nationality;
    Date dob, dod;            // dates of birth & death
    int sex;                  // 0 = female, 1 = male
};
class Student : public Person {
public:
    .
    .
    void printSex() { cout <<(sex ? "male":"female");
}
```

```
protected:
    String id;          // student identification number
    Date dom;           // date of matriculation
    int credits;        // course credits
    float gpa;          // grade-point average
};
```

Now all five data members defined in the `Person` class are accessible from its `Student` subclass, as seen by the following test driver:

```
Student x("Beth Jones", 0, "219360061");
x.setDOB(7, 10, 1983);
x.setDOE(8, 26, 2001);
x.setDOD(7,4,2065);
x.printName();
cout <<"\n    Born: ";   x.printDOB();
cout <<"\n    Sex: ";    x.printSex();
cout <<"\nEntered: ";    x.printDOM();
cout <<endl;
```

```
Beth Jones
    Born: July 10, 1983
    Sex: female
Entered: August 26, 2001
```

The `protected` access category is a balance between `private` and `public` categories: `private` members are accessible only from within the class itself and its `friend` classes; `protected` members are accessible from within the class itself, its `friend` classes, its derived classes, and their `friend` classes; `public` members are accessible from anywhere. In general, `protected` is used instead of `private` whenever it is anticipated that a subclass might be defined for the class.

⭐Note!

A subclass inherits `public` and `protected` members of its base class. From the subclass' view, `public` and `protected` members of its base class appear as though they were declared in the subclass.

If class y is derived from class x, public member a of class x is inherited as a public member of y, and the protected member b of class x is inherited as a protected member of y. But the private member c of class x is not inherited by y.

Overriding and Dominating Inherited Members

If Y is a subclass of X, then Y objects inherit the public and protected member data and methods of X. In the Person, the name data and printName() method are also members of Student.

Sometimes, you might want to define a local version of an inherited member. For example, if a is a data member of X and if Y is a subclass of X, then you could also define a separate data member named a for Y. In this case, we say that the a defined in Y dominates the a defined in X. A reference y.a for an object y of class Y will access the a in Y instead of the a in X. To access the a defined in X, one would use y.X::a.

The same rule applies to methods. If f() is defined in X and another f() with the same signature is defined in Y, then y.f() invokes the latter, and y.X::f() invokes the former. In this case, the local function y.f() overrides the f() function defined in X unless it is invoked as y.X::f().

You Need to Know

In an inheritance hierarchy, default constructors and destructors behave differently from other methods. Each constructor invokes its parent constructor before executing itself, and each destructor invokes its parent destructor after executing itself.

private **Access versus** protected **Access**

The difference between private and protected class members is that subclasses can access protected members of a parent class but not private members. Since protected is more flexible, when would you want to make members private? The answer lies at the heart of the principle of information hiding: restrict access now to facilitate changes later. If you think you may want to modify the implementation of a data member in the future, then declaring it private will obviate the need to make any corollary changes in subclasses.

virtual **Functions and Polymorphism**

One of the most powerful features of C++ is that it allows objects of different types to respond differently to the same function call. This is called *polymorphism* and it is achieved by means of virtual functions. Polymorphism is rendered possible by the fact that a pointer to a base class instance may also point to any subclass instance:

```
class X { . . . }
class Y:public X {// Y is a subclass of x . . . }
main() {
    X* p;    // p - pointer to base class X objects
    Y y;
    p = &y; // p points to subclass Y objects
}
```

If p has type X*, then p can also point to any object whose type is a subclass of X. Even when p is pointing to an instance of a subclass Y, its type is still X*. So an expression like p->f() would invoke the function f() defined in the base class.

Recall that p->f() is an alternative notation for *p.f(). This invokes the member function f() of the object to which p points. But what if p is actually pointing to an object y of a subclass of the class to which p points, and what if that subclass Y has its own overriding version of f()? Which f() gets executed: X::f() or Y::f()? The answer is that p->f() will execute X::f() because p had type X*. The fact that p happens to be pointing at that moment to an instance of subclass Y is irrelevant; it's the <u>statically</u> defined type X* of p that normally determines its behavior.

Example 11.6 Using `virtual` Functions

This demonstration declares p to be a pointer to objects of the base class that point to an instance x of class X. Then it assigns p to point to an instance y

```
class X {
public:
  void f() { cout <<"X::f() executing\n"; }
};
class Y : public X {
public:
  void f() { cout <<"Y::f() executing\n"; }
};
void main() {
  X x;
  Y y;
  X* p = &x;
  p->f();      // invokes X::f() because p has type X*
  p = &y;
  p->f();      // invokes X::f() because p has type X*
}
```

```
X::f() executing
X::f() executing
```
Two function calls p->f() are made. Both calls invoke the same version of f() that is defined in the base class X because p is declared to be a pointer to X objects. Having p point to y has no effect on the second call p->f().

We transform X::f() into a *virtual function* by adding the keyword virtual to its declaration:

```
class X {
public:
    virtual void f() { cout <<"X::f() executing\n"; }
};
```

With the rest of the code left unchanged, the output now becomes:

```
X::f() executing
Y::f() executing
```
Now the second call p->f() invokes Y::f() instead of X::f().

This illustrates *polymorphism:* the <u>same</u> call p->f() invokes <u>different</u> functions. The function is selected according to which class of object p points to. This is called *dynamic binding* because the association *(i.e.,* binding) of the call to the actual code to be executed is deferred until <u>run time</u>. The rule that the pointer's statically defined type determines which member function gets invoked is overruled by declaring the member function virtual.

Essential Point!

Polymorphism is one of the most powerful features of CC++.

Example 11.7 Polymorphism through `virtual` Functions
Here is Person class with Student and Professor subclasses:

```
class Person {
public:
    Person(char* s)
        { name=new char[strlen(s+1)]; strcpy(name, s); }
    void print() {cout <<"I'm " <<name <<".\n";}
protected:
    char* name;
};
class Student : public Person {
public:
    Student(char* s, float g) : Person(s), gpa(g) { }
    void print() { cout <<"I'm " <<name
                        <<" & my GPA is " <<gpa <<".\n";
}
private:
    float gpa;
};
class Professor : public Person {
public:
    Professor(char* s, int n) : Person(s), publs(n) { }
    void print() { cout <<"I'm " <<name
```

```
      <<" & I wrote " <<publs <<" papers.\n"; }
private:
   int publs;
};
void main() {
   Person* p;   Person x("Bob");
   p = &x;        p->print();
   Student y("Tom", 3.47);
   p = &y;        p->print();
   Professor z("Ann", 7);
   p = &z;        p->print();
}
```

```
My name is Bob.
My name is Tom.
My name is Ann.
```

The print() function defined in the base class is not virtual. So the call p -> print() always invokes that same base class function Person::print() because p has type Person*. The pointer p is *statically bound* to that base class function at compile time.

Now change the base class function Person::print() into a virtual function, and run the same program:

```
class Person {
public:
    Person(char* s) { name = new
char[strlen(s+1)];
                        strcpy(name, s); }
    virtual void print()
       { cout <<"I'm " <<name <<"\n"; }
protected:
    char* name;
};
```

```
I'm Bob.
I'm Tom & my GPA is 3.47.
I'm Ann & I wrote 7 papers.
```

Now the pointer p is *dynamically bound* to the print() function of whatever object it points to. The first call p -> print() invokes the base class function Person::print(), the second invokes the derived class function Student::print(), and the third invokes the derived class function Professor::print(). We say that the call p->print() is *polymorphic* because its meaning changes according to circumstance.

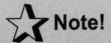

Note!

In general, a member function should be declared as virtual whenever it is anticipated that at least some of its subclasses will define their own local version of the function.

Virtual Destructors

Virtual functions are overridden by functions that have the same signature and are defined in subclasses. Since the names of constructors and destructors involve the names of their different classes, it would seem that constructors and destructors could not be declared virtual. That is indeed true for constructors. However, an exception is made for destructors.

The reason for this exception is that when we instantiate a subclass instance we implicitly invoke base class constructors each of which could allocate memory storage. When we free a subclass we should invoke the destructors of the subclass and all classes on which it is derived.

When a base class destructor is declared virtual, all destructors in a hierarchy will be invoked on the death of an object. This will appropriately free all memory that was allocated by a new operator.

Failure to do this could cause what is known as a *memory leak*. In a large-scale software system, this could lead to a catastrophe. Moreover, it is a bug that is not easily located. The moral is: declare the base class destructor virtual whenever your class hierarchy uses dynamic binding.

Avoid Memory Leaks

Declare your base class destructor virtual if you use dynamic binding!

Chapter 12
STREAM I/O

IN THIS CHAPTER:

✔ *Stream Classes*
✔ *The* ios *Class*
✔ ios *State Variables*
✔ *The* istream *and*
   ostream *Classes*
✔ *Unformatted Input Functions*
✔ *Unformatted Output Functions*
✔ *Stream Manipulators*

Stream Classes

The C++ programming language does not include any input/output facilities. These are supplied by using standard libraries. We have used the directive #include <iostream.h> in every program that does I/O. This includes the iostream.h header file that includes the definitions for the I/O library function. This chapter describes in more detail the contents of this library and how it is used.

The I/O library defines a hierarchies of *stream classes.*

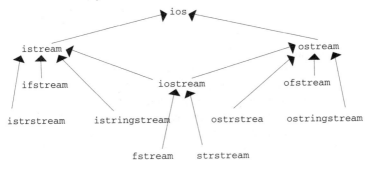

The iostream class is the one that we usually use for ordinary I/O. Note that it is a subclass of both the `istream` and the `ostream` classes, both of which are subclasses of the `ios` base class. The classes with "fstream" in their name are used for file processing.

The `ios` Class

The `ios` class serves as the base class for the other stream classes. Its primary purpose is to control the buffer for whatever stream object has been instantiated. This means that the stream controls how many characters are inserted into or extracted from the buffer. To do that, the `ios` object maintains a collection of data elements that control I/O behavior. They include such things as the number base (octal, decimal, hexadecimal) that is used, the width of the display field, the number of digits displayed for floating point numbers, etc. We shall examine how to interface with the `ios` class.

`ios` State Variables

Every stream has a _state data member that is defined in the ios class. The _state member is a bit string that holds several Boolean variables. These *state variables* are specified in the enum definition:

```
enum { goodbit=0,        // all ok
```

```
eofbit  = 01,   // end of file
failbit = 02,   // last operation failed
badbit  = 04    // invalid operation
};
```

A stream's format flags can only be changed explicitly, and only by means of the access functions described below. In contrast, a stream's state variables are changed implicitly, a result of I/O operations. For example, when a user inputs **Control-Z** to indicate end-of-file, the cin's *eof flag* is set, and we say that the stream is an *eof state*.

A stream's four state variables (goodbit, eofbit, failbit, and badbit) can be accessed individually by their access functions (good(), eof(), fail(), and bad()). State variables are generally used to read the current state of the stream. The stream conversion operator () is overloaded to return 0 if the state is nonzero. So for example, if in is an input stream, then the expression (in) will evaluate to true if none of the flags are set (i.e., there is still more input), and false otherwise.

The second of these access functions overloads the negation operator. It simply calls fail() and returns its return value, which will be nonzero unless both the failbit and the badbit are clear. The advantage of this alternate form for determining whether the stream can be used any more is that, like the conversion operator above, this form can be used conveniently in conditional expressions.

Example 12.1 Operator `operator void*()` for Loop Control

```
int n, sum = 0; cin >> n;
while (cin) {  // loop continues while _state
    sum += n;   cin >> n;
}
```

```
44  11  22
^z
sum = 77
```

Using **Control-Z** to terminate input is simple and convenient. Pressing this key sets the eofbit in the input stream. If you want to use it again in the program, it has to be cleared first. This is done with the member function clear(), as: cin.clear();

The `istream` and `ostream` Classes

The `istream` and `ostream` classes both inherit from the `ios` class:

```
class istream : virtual public ios { // . . . };
class ostream : virtual public ios { // . . .
```

Making `ios` a virtual base class facilitates the multiple inheritance that the `iostream` class has from both the `istream` and `ostream` classes by preventing multiple copies of the `ios` class to be made for the `iostream` class.

The `istream` class defines the `cin` object and the stream extraction operator `>>` for *formatted input*. The `ostream` class defines the `cout`, `cerr`, and `clog` objects and the stream insertion operator `<<` for *formatted output*.

The familiar I/O operations that use the extraction and insertion operators are called *formatted I/O* because they recognize the types of the objects accessed and format the data accordingly. For example, if n is an integer with value 22, then `cout << n` prints the value 22 in integer format. The `istream` and `ostream` classes also define a set of member functions for *unformatted I/O* desribed briefly in the next section that handles data simply as a sequence of bytes.

The `istream` class defines the stream extraction operator `>>` which reads data from `istream` objects, which are usually the standard input device cin (*i.e.*, the keyboard). If successful, this operator returns a reference to the object so that calls can be chained like

```
cin >> x >> y >> z;
```

If `cin` is unsuccessful, it returns 0. Under normal operation, `cin` skips white space characters (blanks, tabs, newlines, *etc.*). The `>>` operator will return 0 when it encounters the end-of-file character. This can be used to control an input loop:

Example 12.2 Controlling an Input Loop

```
int n, sum = 0;
while (cin >> n) sum += n;
cout <<"The sum is " <<sum <<endl;
```

```
80 70 60 50 40 30 20 10 ^Z
The sum is 360
```

Unformatted Input Functions

The `istream` class defines a rich collection of unformatted input functions. Several versions of the `get()` function are defined by the `istream` class. In its simplest form, it has no arguments and simply returns the next character in the input stream. Its function prototype is `int get();`. This version of the function is typically used in an input loop as shown by the following fragment:

```
char c;
while ((c=cin.get())!=EOF) cout <<c;
cout <<endl;
```

```
What is in a name?
What is in a name?
I don't know!
I don't know!
^D
```

Each call of the `cin.get()` function reads one more character from `cin` and returns it to the variable c. Then the statement inside the loop inserts c into the output stream. These characters accumulate in a buffer until the end-of-line character is inserted. Then the buffer is flushed, and the complete line is printed just as it had been read.

The expression `(c=cin.get())` returns a value that is compared with the integer constant EOF. As long as they are unequal, the loop continues. When the end-of-file character `^D` is read, `cin.get()` returns the value of EOF (usually –1), thereby terminating the loop.

Another form of the `get()` function reads the next character from the input stream into its reference char parameter:

```
istream& get(char& c);
```

This version returns false when the end of file is detected, so it can conveniently be used to control an input loop. The previous loop control could be equivalently rewritten:

```
while (cin.get(ch))
```

A third form of the `get()` function is similar to the `getline()` function. Its prototype is

```
istream& get(char* buf, int n, char delim='\n');
```

This reads characters into `buf` until either `n-1` characters are read or the `delim` character is encountered, whichever comes first. It does <u>not</u> extract `delim` from the input stream.

The `getline()` function is almost the same as the third form of the `get()` function. The only difference is that it <u>does</u> extract the delimiter character from the input stream but does not store it in the buf. Its prototype is

```
istream& getline(char* buf, int n, char delim='\n');
```

The `ignore()` function is used to "eat" characters in the input stream. It simply extracts characters, without copying them into any variable. Its prototype is

```
istream& ignore(int n=1, int delim=EOF);
```

In its simplest form, `cin.ignore()` extracts one character from `cin`. More generally, `cin.ignore(n)` will extract n characters from `cin`, and `cin.ignore(100000, '$')` would extract all the characters up to and including the next `'$'` character (or to the end of the file).

Unformatted Output Functions

The `istream` class defines functions for unformatted output that are analogous to unformatted input functions. The two versions of the `put()` function are the inverses of the corresponding `get()` functions:

```
int put(char c);
ostream& put(char c);
```

They both insert the character c into the output stream.

Example 12.3 Using the `cout.put()` Function
This example shows the parallel nature of `put()` and `get()`:

```
char c;
while (cin.get(c)) cout.put(c);
cout <<endl;
```

```
The woods are lovely, dark and deep.
The woods are lovely, dark and deep.
But I have promises to keep,
But I have promises to keep,
^D
```

The `write()` function has versions that are the inverses of the corresponding read functions:

```
ostream& write(const char* buf, int n);
ostream& write(const unsigned char* buf, int n);
```

They both transfer n bytes from buf to the output stream.

Stream Manipulators

A *stream manipulator* is a special kind of stream class member function. When used with the insertion and extraction operators, they look like objects. They really are function calls. For example, cout <<endl; is actually a call to the stream manipulator function endl(). When operator<< is invoked, it is done so with a pointer pointing to the cout.endl() function. After printing the newline it returns a pointer to cout.

So cout <<x <<y is actually processed as (cout <<x) <<y. After the cout <<x is processed it evaluates to a reference to cout which in turn evaluates cout <<y. The next example shows how you can write your own stream manipulator.

Example 12.4 A "Home-Grown" Stream Manipulator

```
ostrearn& beep(ostrearn& ostr) {
   return ostr <<"\a";
}
void main() {
   cout <<beep;
}
```

When used as shown here, the stream manipulator sends the *alert character* '\a' to the output stream which sounds the *system beep*.

All stream manipulators work this way. They are defined with prototypes like this:

```
        ios& f(ios& ostr)
        ostream& f(ostream& ostr)
        istream& f(ostream& istr)
```

or, in the case of manipulators with parameters, like this:

```
        ios& f(ios& ostr, int n)
        ostream& f(ostream& ostr, int n)
        istream& f(ostream& istr, int n)
```

Table 12.1 lists of some of the more common stream manipulators.

Table 12.1 Stream Manipulators

Manipulator	Stream	Action
binary	ios	Set stream mode to binary

`dec`	ios	Read-write integers base 10 (default)
`endl`	ostream	End output line and flush output stream
`ends`	ostream	End output string
`flush`	ostream	Flush output stream
`hex`	ios	Read/write integers base 16
`oct`	ios	Read/write integers base 8)
`resetiosflags(long u`	ios	Clear format flags specified by u
`setbase(int n)`	ostream	Write integers base n (default: 10)
`setfill(int ch)`	ostream	Set fill character to ch (default: ' '}
`setiosflags(long u)`	ios	Set format flags specified by u
`Setprecision(int n)`	ios	Set floating point precision = n digits (default: 6)
`setw(int n)`	ios	Set field width to n columns (default: 0)
`text`	ios	Set stream to text (default)
`ws`	istream	Skip white space

We have already seen how the `endl` manipulator works. It inserts the newline character '\n' into the output stream and then calls the `flush` manipulator which "flushes" the buffer.

The `ends` manipulator simply inserts the null character '\0' into the output stream.

The `oct`, `dec`, `hex`, and `setbase(n)` manipulators are used to change the number base integers that are input or output.

Example 12.5 Using the oct, dec, and hex Stream Manipulators

```
int n = 510;
cout << "Hexadecimal:" <<hex <<n <<endl;
cout << "    Decimal:" <<dec <<n <<endl;
cout << "      Octal:" <<oct <<n <<endl;
cout <<"Enter integer in octal: ";
cin >>oct >>n;    // read integer  base 8
```

The first three `cout` statements would display n in hexadecimal, decimal, and octal. The `cin` statement would change input to be in octal. Recall that the manipulator resets the number base for all subsequent input or output until another manipulator is used.

The `ws` manipulator simply eats the next string of white space (blanks, tabs, newlines).

Appendix A
C++ KEYWORDS

C++ has 48 keywords. These special words are used to define the syntax of the language.

Keyword	Description	Example
asm	Allows information to be passed to the assembler directly	`asm ("check");`
auto	Storage class for objects that exist only within their own block	`auto int n;`
break	Terminates a loop or a `switch` statement	`break;`
case	Used in a `switch` statement to specify control expression	`switch (n/10)`
catch	Specifies actions to take when an exception occurs	`catch(error)`
char	An integer type	`char c;`
class	Specifies a class declaration	`class X {...};`
const	Specifies a constant definition	`const int s=32;`
continue	Jumps to beginning of next iteration in a loop	`continue;`
default	The "otherwise" case in a `switch` statement	`default: sum=0;`
delete	Deallocates memory allocated by a new statement	`delete a;`
do	Specifies a `do . . . while` loop	`do {...} while`
double	A real number type	`double x;`
else	Specifies alternative in an if statement	`else n = 0;`
enum	Used to declare an enumeration type	`enum bool {...}`
extern	Storage class for objects declared outside the local block	`extern int max;`
float	A real number type	`float x;`
for	Specifies a for loop	`for ( ; ; ) ...`
friend	Specifies a friend function in a class	`friend int f();`

goto	Causes execution to jump to a labeled statement	goto error;
if	Specifies an if statement	if (n>0) …
inline	Declares a function whose text is to be substituted for its call	inline int f()
int	An integer type	int n;
long	Used to define integer and real types	long double x;
new	Allocates memory	int* p=new int;
operator	Used to declare an operator overload	X operator++();
private	Specifies private declarations in a class	private: int n;
protected	Specifies protected declarations in a class	protected:int n;
public	Specifies public declarations in a class	public: int n;
register	Storage class specifier for objects stored in registers	register int i;
return	Statement that terminates a function and returns a value	return 0;
short	An integer type	short n;
signed	Used to define integer types	signed char c;
sizeof	Operator that returns the number of bytes used to store an object	n=sizeof(float);
static	Storage class of objects that exist for the duration of the program	static int n;
struct	Specifies a structure definition	struct X {…};
switch	Specifies a switch statement	switch (n){…}
template	Specifies a template class	Template <class T>
this	Pointer that points to the current object	return *this;
throw	Used to generate an exception	throw X();
try	Specifies a block that contains exception handlers	try {…}
typedef	Declares a synonym for an existing type	typedef int Num;
union	Specifies a structure whose elements occupy the same storage	union z {…};
unsigned	Used to define integer types	unsigned int b;
virtual	Declares a member function that is defined in a subclass	virtual int f();
void	Designates the absence of a type	void f();
volatile	Declares objects that can be modified outside of program control	int volatile n;
While	Specifies a while loop	while (n>0)…

Appendix B
C++ OPERATORS

This table lists all the C++ operators, grouped by order of precedence. The higher-level precedence operators are evaluated before the lower-level precedence operators. For example, in the expression (a - b * c), the * operator will be evaluated first and the - operator second, because * has precedence level 13 which is higher than the level 12 precedence of -. The column labeled "As" tells whether an operator is right (R) or left (L) associative. The expression (a-b-c) is evaluated as ((a - b) - c) because - is left associative. The column labeled "Ar" tells whether an operator operates on one, two, or three operands (unary (1), binary (2), or ternary (3)). The column labeled "Ov" tells whether an operator is overloadable. (*See* Chapter 8.)

Op	Name	Pr	As	Ar	Ov	Example
::	Global scope resolution	17	R	1	N	::x
::	Class scope resolution	17	L	2	N	X::x
.	Direct member selection	16	L	2	N	s.len
->	Indirect member selection	16	L	2	Y	p->len
[ ]	Subscript	16	L	2	Y	a[i]
( )	Function call	16	L	n/a	Y	rand()
( )	Type construction	16	L	n/a	Y	int(ch)
++	Post-increment	16	R	1	Y	n++
–	Post-decrement	16	R	1	Y	n–
sizeof	Size of object or type	15	R	1	N	sizeof(a)
++	Pre-increment	15	R	1	Y	++n
–	Pre-decrement	15	R	1	Y	–n
~	Bitwise complement	15	R	1	Y	~s
!	Logical NOT	15	R	1	Y	!p
+	1 plus	15	R	1	Y	+n
–	1 minus	15	R	1	Y	-n
*	Dereference	15	R	1	Y	*p

&	Address	15	R	1	Y	&x
new	Allocation	15	R	1	Y	new p
delete	Deallocation	15	R	1	Y	delete p
( )	Type conversion	15	R	2	Y	int(ch)
.*	Direct member selection	14	L	2	N	x.*q
->*	Indirect member selection	14	L	2	Y	p->q
*	Multiplicaion	13	L	2	Y	m*n
/	Division	13	L	2	Y	m/n
%	Remainder	13	L	2	Y	m%n
+	Addition	12	L	2	Y	m+n
-	Subtraction	12	L	2	Y	m-n
<<	Bit shift left	11	L	2	Y	cout << n
>>	Bit shift right	11	L	2	Y	cin >> n
<	Less than	10	L	2	Y	x < y
<=	Less than or equal to	10	L	2	Y	x <= y
>	Greater than	10	L	2	Y	x > y
>=	Greater than or equal to	10	L	2	Y	x >= y
==	Equal to	9	L	2	Y	x == y
!=	Nt equal to	9	L	2	Y	x != y
&	Bitwise AND	8	L	2	Y	s&t
^	Bitwise XOR	7	L	2	Y	s^t
|	Bitwise OR	6	L	2	Y	s|t
&&	Logical AND	5	L	2	Y	u && v
||	Logical OR	4	L	2	Y	u || v
?:	Conditional expression	3	L	3	N	u ? x:y
=	Assignment	2	R	2	Y	n = 22
+=	Addition assignment	2	R	2	Y	n += 8
-=	Subtraction assignment	2	R	2	Y	n - = 4
*=	Multiplication assignment	2	R	2	Y	n *= -1
/=	Division assignment	2	R	2	Y	n /= 10
%=	Remainder assignment	2	R	2	Y	n %= 10
&=	Bitwise AND assignment	2	R	2	Y	s &= mask
^=	Bitwise XOR assignment	2	R	2	Y	s ^= mask
|=	Bitwise OR assignment	2	R	2	Y	s |= mask
<<=	Bit shift left assignment	2	R	2	Y	s <<= 1
>>=	Bit shift right assignment	2	R	2	Y	s >>= 1
,	Comma	0	L	2	Y	++m, -n

Appendix C
PRE-DEFINED
FUNCTIONS

Describes functions provided in the C++ libraries.

Function <header> Example & Brief Description

abort() <stdlib.h> void abort(); Aborts the program.

abs() <stdlib.h> int abs(int n); Absolute value of n.

acos() <math.h> double acos(double x); Inverse cosine (arccosine) of x.

asin() <math.h> double asin(double x); Inverse sine (arcsine) of x.

atan() <math.h> double atan(double x); Inverse tangent (arctangent) of x.

atof() <stdlib.h> double atof(const char* s); Returns floating-point number represented in string s.

atoi() <stdlib.h> int atoi(const char* s); Returns integer represented in string s.

atol() <stdlib.h> long atol(const char* s); Returns integer represented in string s.

bad() <iostream.h> int ios::bad(); Returns nonzero if badbit is set; returns 0 otherwise.

bsearch() <stdlib.h> void* bsearch(const void* x, void* a, size_t n, size-t s, (*cmp)(const void*, const void*)); Implements binary search to search for x in the sorted array a of n elements of size s using the function *cmp to compare elements. If found, a pointer to the element is returned; otherwise, NULL is returned

ceil() <math.h> double ceil(double x); Returns x rounded up to the next whole number.

clear() <iostream.h> void ios::clear(int n=0); Changes stream state to n.

clearerr() <stdio.h> void clearerr(FILE* p); Clears end-of-file and error flags for the file *p.

162

close() <fstream.h> void fstreambase::close(); Closes the file attached to the owner object.

cos() <math.h> double cos(double x); Inverse cosine of x.

cosh() <math.h> double cosh(double x); Hyperbolic cosine of x: $(e^x + e^{-x})/2$.

difftime() <time.h> double difftime(time-t t1, time_t t0); Returns time elapsed (in seconds) from time t0 to time t1

eof() <iostream.h> int ios::eof(); Returns nonzero if eofbit is set; Returns 0 otherwise.

exit() <stdlib.h> void exit(int n); Terminates program & returns n to the invoking process

exp() <math.h> double exp(double x); Exponential of x: e^x.

fabs() <math.h> double fabs(double x); Absolute value of x.

fail() <iostream.h> int ios::fail(); Returns nonzero if failbit is set; Returns 0 otherwise.

fclose() <stdio.h> int fclose(FILE* p); Closes the file *p and flushes all buffers. Returns 0 if successful; returns EOF otherwise.

fgetc() <stdio.h> int fgetc(FILE* p); Reads & returns next character from the *p if possible; else returns EOF.

fgets() <stdio.h> char* fgets(char* s, int n, FILE* P); Reads the next line from the file *p and stores it in *s. The "next line" means either the next n-1 characters or all the characters up to the next endline character, whichever comes first. The NUL is appended to the characters stored in s. Returns s if successful; returns NULL otherwise.

fill() <iostream.h> char ios::fill(); Returns current fill character. char ios::fill(char c) ; Changes fill char to c and returns previous fill character.

flags() <iostream.h> long ios::flags(); Returns the current format flags. long ios::flags(long n); Changes format flags to n; returns previous flags.

floor() <math.h> double floor(double x); Returns x rounded down to the next whole number.

flush() <iostream.h> ostream& ostream::flush();Flushes the output buffer and returns the updates stream.

fopen() <iostream.h> FILE* fopen(const char* p, const char* s); Opens file *p and returns address of the file structure if successful; else returns NULL. String s sets file's *mode:* "r" = *read,* "w" = *write,* "a" = *append,* "r+" or "w+" = reading and writing an existing file, and "a+" = reading and appending an existing file.

fprintf() <iostream.h> int fprintf(FILE* p, const char* s); Writes formatted output to the file * p. Returns the number of characters printed if successful; otherwise it returns a negative number.

putc() `<stdio.h>` `int fputc(int c, FILE* p);` Writes character c to the file * p. Returns the character written or EOF if unsuccessful.

fputs() `<iostream.h>` `int fputs(const char* s, FILE* p);` Writes string s to the file *p. Returns a nonnegative integer if successful; otherwise it returns EOF

fread() `<iostream.h>` `size-t fread(void* s, size_t k, size_t n, FILE* p);` Reads up to n items each of size k from the file *p and stores them at location s in memory. Returns the number of items read

fscanf() `<iostream.h>` `int fscanf(FILE* p, const char* s);` Reads formatted input from the file *p and stores it at location. Returns EOF if end of file; otherwise returns the number of items read.

fseek() `<iostream.h>` `int fseek(FILE* p, long k, int base);` Repositions the position marker of the file *p k bytes from its base, where base should be SEEK_SET for the beginning of the file, SEEK_CUR for the current position of the file marker or SEEK_END for the end of the file. Returns 0 if successful.

ftell() `<iostream.h>` `long ftell(FILE* p);` Returns the location of the position marker in file *p or returns-1.

fwrite() `<iostream.h>` `size-t fwrite(void* s, size-t k, size-t n, FILE* p);` Writes n items each of size k to the file *p and Returns the number written.

gcount() `<stdio.h>` `int istream::gcount();` Returns the number of characters most recently read.

get() `<stdio.h>` `int istream::get(); istream& istream::get (signed char& c); istream& istream::get(unsigned char& c); istream& istream::get(signed char* b, int n, char e='\n'); istream& istream::get(unsigned char* b, int n, char e=,\n');` Reads the next character c from the istream. The first version returns c or EOF. The last two versions read up to n characters into b, stopping when e is encountered.

getc() `<stdio.h>` `int getc(FILE* p);` Same as `fgetc()` except implemented as a macro.

getchar() `<stdio.h>` `int getchar();` Returns the next character from standard input or returns EOF.

gets() `<stdio.h>` `char* gets(char* s);` Reads next line from standard input and stores it in s. Returns s or NULL if no characters are read.

good() `<iostream.h>` `int ios::good();` Returns nonzero if stream state is zero; returns zero otherwise.

ignore() `<iostream.h>` `istream& ignore(int n=1, int e=EOF);` Extracts up to n characters from stream, or up to character e, which ever comes first. Returns the stream.

isalnum() `<ctype.h>` `int isalnum(int c);` Returns nonzero if c is an alphabetic or numeric character; returns 0 otherwise.

isalpha() `<ctype.h> int isalpha(int c);` Returns nonzero if c is an alphabetic character; otherwise returns 0.

iscntrl() `<ctype.h> int iscntrl(int c);` Returns nonzero if c is a control character; otherwise returns 0.

isdigit() `<ctype.h> int isdigit(int c);` Returns nonzero if c is a digit character; otherwise returns 0.

isgraph() `<ctype.h> int isgraph(int c);` Returns nonzero if c is any non-blank printing character; otherwise returns 0.

islower() `<ctype.h> int islower(int c);` Returns nonzero if c is a lowercase alphabetic character; otherwise returns 0.

isprint() `<ctype.h> int isprint(int c);` Returns nonzero if c is any printing character; otherwise returns 0.

ispunct() `<ctype.h> int ispunct(int c);` Returns nonzero if c is any punctuation mark, except the alphabetic characters, the numeric characters, and the blank; otherwise returns 0.

isspace() `<ctype.h> int isspace(int c);` Returns nonzero if c is a white-space character, including the blank, the form feed the newline, the carriage return, the horizontal tab, and the vertical tab; otherwise returns 0.

isupper() `<ctype.h> int isupper(int c);` Returns nonzero if c is an uppercase alphabetic character; otherwise returns 0.

isxdigit() `<ctype.h> int isxdigit(int c);` Returns nonzero if c is one of the 10 digit characters or one of the 12 hexadecimal digit letters: 'a', 'b', 'c', 'd', 'e', 'f', 'A', 'B', 'C', 'D', 'E', or 'F'; otherwise Returns 0.

labs() `<stdlib.h> long labs(long n);` Absolute value of n.

log() `<math.h> double log(double x);` Natural logof x.

log10() `<math.h> double log10(double x);` Common log of x.

memchr() `<string.h> void* memchr(const void* s, int c, size-t k);` Searches k bytes of memory beginning at s for character c. If found, the address of its first occurrence is returned; NULL otherwise.

memcmp() `<string.h> int memcmp(const void* s1, const void* s2, size-t k);` Compares the k bytes of memory beginning at s1 with the k bytes of memory beginning at s2 and returns a negative, zero, or a positive integer according to whether the first string is lexicographically less than, equal to, or greater than the second string.

memcpy() `<string.h> void* memcpy(const void* s1, const void* s2, size-t k);` Copies the k bytes of memory beginning at s2 into memory location s1 and returns s1.

memmove() `<string.h> int memmove(const void* s1, const void* s2, size-t k);` Same as memcpy() except strings may overlap.

open() `<fstream.h> void fstream::open(const char* f, int m, int p=filebuf::openprot); void ifstream::open(const char* f, int m=ios::in, int p=filebuf::openprot); void ofstream`

`::open(const char* f, int m=ios::out, int p=filebuf::open-prot);` Opens the file f in mode m with protection p.

peek() `<iostream.h> int istream:: peek();` Returns next character (or EOF) from stream without extracting it.

pow() `<math h> double pow(double x, double y);` Returns x raised to the power y (x^y).

precision() `<iostream.h> int ios::precision(); int ios::precision(int k);` Returns the precision for the stream. The second version changes the precision to k and returns the old precision.

tolower() `<ctype.h> int tolower(int c);` Returns the lowercase version of c if c is an uppercase alphabetic character; otherwise returns c.

toupper() `<ctype.h> int toupper(int c);` Returns the uppercase version of c if c is an lowercase alphabetic character; otherwise returns c.

Index